Caesar's Gladiator Pit
By
Aubran "Buddy" Martin

"Early I woke to the
sound of loud screaming noise. . . ."

CAESAR'S GLADIATOR PIT

By

BUDDY MARTIN

Illustrations by BOB CUNNINGHAM,
RON CONNOLLY, & BUDDY MARTIN

Poems by THOMAS G. NICKENS,
& BUDDY MARTIN

Cover by BUDDY MARTIN

TOWER PRESS
Hollidaysburg, PA 16635

FIRST PRINTING   Spring, 1985

ISBN: 0-932153-00-3
Library of Congress Catalog Card Number: 85-51047

TOWER PRESS
410 Penn Street
Hollidaysburg, PA   16648

Printed in the United States of America

PREFACE

Caesar's Gladiator Pit is the first of a series of books intended to provide a legitimate forum for the ideas and perspectives of the most downtrodden class of citizens in society - that of prison inmates. It is to this group of social outcasts that Tower Press turns to provide new insights into social life itself, as well as to offer information and suggest solutions to one of the most perplexing problems of modern industrial society, that of the growing number of prisons and prisoners.

It is perhaps a novel approach to treat prison inmates as experts. This perspective certainly conflicts with current penal practice which confines and isolates inmates and gags their every attempt for self-expression. This perspective also runs counter to the average citizens' sentiment that those who break the law should be ostracized and punished for their crimes. Why then the need for Tower Press?

The idea for this type of endeavor grew out of my personal involvement in the education of inmates at the maximum security state penitentiary in Huntingdon, Pennsylvania. It was at this facility nearly

PREFACE

ten years ago where I worked as an instructor in sociology for Penn State University and had as students hundreds of inmates, as well as dozens of law enforcement personnel. It was through talking and listening to these men who were most intimately involved and effected by the prison environment that led me to the conclusion that the present system of incarceration was unproductive, inefficient, and essentially an enormous waste of public funds.

This is not to say that prisons are not doing well that which they are expected to do. Today's prisons, probably better than at any time in the past, are well equipped; run by professionally trained staff; and organized so that they very effectively house, control, and isolate hundreds, and in the case of larger institutions, thousands of inmates. This they do very well. But while they get an excellent grade for institutionalizing large numbers of people, they flunk miserably by releasing to society men and women who are bitter, angry, socially ill-equipped for readjusting to society, and, of concern to us all, more likely to break the law again and engage in many destructive forms of anti-social behavior. Prisons, when evaluated from the perspective of rehabilitation and measured by current rates of recidivism, have to be listed as social failures.

This, then, brings us to the core of the current debate concerning prisons and prison reform. Prison, as a social institution, is certainly needed to incarcerate and set apart from society those individuals who have been

PREFACE

found to be destructive or dangerous. Admittedly, prison is also needed to serve as a deterrant to those who might otherwise take unfair advantage if not faced with the threat of punishment. These ideas form the bedrock upon which prisons were founded. But the hard-core penologist must also recognize the well-documented social facts that point to prisons, reformatories, and jails as causes, rather than cures, for the high rates of crime among ex-offenders.

Taken collectively, the average inmate is a product of the streets. He is usually poor, has grown up in a series of institutions, is a school dropout, and is functionally illiterate. He is very likely to be a member of a social minority and a member of a lower-class subculture. These attributes of inmates are well-documented and serve as the basis for explaining the causes of criminal behavior. What is not so well-documented is the high level of personal knowledge gained by inmates through years of individual involvement and social interaction with every facet of the criminal justice system. If sociologists have been so successful at explaining crime by studying the lives of criminals, why can't we also learn why prisons fail by studying the lives of prisoners? It is from this perspective that this series of books and monographs is presented.

Through my years of teaching in prison I was fortunate to have had as students several inmates who have spent lifetimes in prison and shared in their belief that there must be a better way. These men could not be classified as typical. These were convicts who were willing to study and learn. These were men who had evolved through a life of crime and institutionalization and were now perceptive to the social forces and patterns which molded their lives. These were inmates who sought a positive future and dared to break the social bonds which tied them to the endless cycle of crime and imprisonment. These were also men who intimately understood the interworkings of the prison environment and who sought to do whatever they could to facilitate change so that others who were younger and less experienced would not have to share their fate. Aubran W. Martin was one of these inmates.

From the first time we met, "Buddy" Martin demonstrated an intense desire to learn, a craving for knowledge, and a dedication to artistic pursuits that was truly astounding. Once I got to know Buddy, the crime he was accused of, and the three life sentences he faced, I understood why.

Prior to his conviction for the killing of the Yablonskis, Buddy Martin was a tough street kid who had matured physically but still suffered from the emotional and psychological scars of a life of family strife, poverty, institutionalization, and loneliness. To make it in the world Buddy knew you had to be tough. And tough he was. Buddy's reputation in the streets of Cleveland was that he was fearless, daring, and out to make a buck; these being the kinds of attributes that gains one admission into the inner circle of organized crime.

PREFACE

Buddy had supported himself as a burglar since his early teens. But it was not until after he had spent years in reformatories and had failed to hold several legitimate jobs that he began to see himself as a professional burglar. It was at this time that he gained admission into the burglary ring that was to get him caught up in the series of events that was to lead to the assassination of Jock Yablonski and his family.

The account of what happened the night of the murders differs among the three men involved. Buddy, from the time of his arrest, swears that he never knew of a murder plot. To him, the mission that night was no different from others he had participated in with his fellow burglars. His job was to stay with the car and serve as a lookout while the other two went into the house to secure what was suspected to be a $50,000 coin collection. Although most of the evidence was circumstantial, it was the testimony of one of the other burglars that got Buddy Martin convicted of three murders and sentenced to prison for the rest of his life. Regardless of the outcome of the trial and the labeling of Buddy Martin by the media as a professional "hit man," and a hired assassin, there are only three people who actually know what happened that night.

When I first met Buddy, the Supreme Court was deciding whether or not he could be legally executed for the murders. Needless to say, this was a time of personal anguish for Buddy Martin. Although hardship is never pleasant nor desirable, it can serve in some

PREFACE

as a turning point, an acceptance of new values and pursuits, a time of personal and individual change. Changes were certainly evident in the life of Buddy Martin; changes that were directed toward the intense desire to understand, to communicate, and to be heard - Buddy Martin had become an artist.

The rough draft of this story of Caesar's Gladiator Pit was written in thirty-two days. It begins and ends in prison. It tells of an endless cycle of loneliness and despair that characterizes too many of the young lives of those who occupy the reformatories, jails and prisons of contemporary society. It is presented with the hope that society will focus its constructive and creative talent on an institution and an attitude that has gone unchanged for thousands of years.

Ted Alleman, President
Tower Press

THE AUTHOR

Aubran "Buddy" Martin is presently incarcerated at the State Correctional Institution in Huntingdon, Pennsylvania. He was born May 7, 1948 in Madison, West Virginia. Buddy is one of seven children. At the age of seven he moved with his family from a rural mountain hollow in West Virginia to the inner city of Cleveland, Ohio.

At the age of twenty-three, Buddy Martin was sentenced to die in the electric chair. He spent two years in solitary confinement and began his education through reading. He developed a serious interest in art when he was assigned a job in the institution's craft shop. He soon demonstrated promise as an artist by winning several first prize honors. His art has since been critically acclaimed nationwide and has been exhibited in art galleries in Pennsylvania and Texas.

Buddy's interest in art soon led to a personal drive for self-education. Beginning at little more than the seventh grade level, he became an avid reader and took advantage of whatever formal education was offered by the institution. After years of study, he attained his high school diploma and went on to earn an Associate Degree in Sociology from the Pennsylvania State University.

Buddy Martin's interest in writing developed nearly two years ago as a response to the mounting pressure from the prison administration to limit many of his artistic endeavors. Buddy's writing, like his art, is reflective of the personal crisis he faces, and the prison environment in which he lives. His avowed goal is to develop a positive and constructive future for himself, while fighting for the right to prove his claim of innocence in a court of law. His criminal convictions have been under appeal for the past twelve years.

Constructive comment and correspondence is welcome and can be addressed personally to A. W. Martin (P-1176), Drawer R, Huntingdon, PA 16652.

CREDITS

As human beings, when caught up in the perception of human achievement, we tend to look only at the individual who concludes the expressive statement of that achievement. We never see the coach who stands in the unrecognizable background. We never see the multiple social forces that hammer, bend, mold, weld, forge, and discipline that person so he can attain the state of excellence. From many people I've learned man cannot achieve any sense of greatness without the influential force of a caring neighbor.

Dr. Stephen Grout, you came and offered assistance when I sat in a dark and cold shadow. I was underneath the sharp and insensitive blade of Caesar's execution ax. I sat there, deeply in fear, and waiting to die. You offered me an artist's paint brush. When you did, compared to the reality I knew, I thought you were insane and I was deeply aggravated by you annoying me with such bizarre foolishness.

But with that gift you laid down a magic, creative stone that gave my life a foundation on which to build. The energy that flowed through the paint of that brush turned my bottled-up expressions into that of a highly charged conductor of creativity. How could I have known, then, that you offered me such tremendous and awesome power? How could I have known, then, that I would seek out the riddles, the beauty, of the unknown universe through the channels of that paint brush? I want to deeply thank you, Steve, for having the compassion and courage to care for a wounded, rejected, and dying young man. I want to thank you for becoming my close friend and teacher over the many long and difficult years.

Ted Alleman, you too extended to me your deep human concern as I sat amid the uncertain shadows waiting to die. As a sociology instructor for Penn State University, you walked into this isolated prison environment and taught me as much as you could. At that point in my life I was lost and thought that I had been abandoned by humanity. You taught me theories about the nature of social and individual behavior. And when you learned I was waiting to be executed and that I was emotionally and intellectually confused you said to me, "Buddy, before you can do anything for yourself you have to get your head together."

With patience, fortitude, compassion, and human concern you helped me heal. You cultivated me and helped me grow. You taught me how to research, analyze, expand, develop and achieve levels of human success that was far beyond my hope or the grasp of my imagination. Now I know why the slave master did not want the black man to learn how to read. He would become too independent and competitive if he learned that magic. He would ask too many questions and eventually learn, truly, he was not someone's nigger.

This manuscript of Caesar's Gladiator Pit is, to a great extent, a document that could never have been developed without your guidance and human concern. Ted, you are a man of whom this world should be proud. I want to thank you for being my friend, companion, and for supplying me with great motivating dreams. You have given me a tremendous amount of hope and a positive force with which to battle the darkness of this prison environment. You have given me a positive outlook on life. There could never be a greater gift to any man.

Missy McKai Cartier, I thank you for your many years of encouragement and faithful friendship. You were a disc-jocky at WQWK in State College, Pennsylvania and you played music once a week for the imprisoned people. I met you when you came to be a guest speaker at a prison banquet. When you asked me what I was doing in prison I told you a lie. I didn't want to frighten you by telling you I had three death sentences. I was afraid you would run away from me.

I deceived you for awhile but eventually you discovered the truth. However, you did not run. Instead, you bonded to me closer. I watched you struggle as you tugged at my heavy chains. I watched the emotional conflict rip and tear at your youthful spirit. But I also watched you pull out your sword and flash it through the air when people slandered me or tried to attack me.

We each had our problems and together we struggled to make each other strong. In your spirit I saw a psychic butterfly along with fantasies and stuff. Thank you, Missy, for never abandoning me. You have been a real good friend. And now, even over the thousands of miles of separation, you still reach back to touch me; to tell me I have a friend. Thank you, Missy. You are a very special person.

I thank Dr. Malcolm Hill of Penn State University for his creative idea of using one of my drawings as the design for the book cover. I also thank Grace Coveney for her invaluable assistance with the editing and typing of the manuscript.

In addition, Ron Connolly and Bob Cunningham deserve special thanks for their courage in allowing me to use several of their controversial illustrations for Caesar's Gladiator Pit. Too, I thank Thomas G. Nickens for the use of his excellent poem titled, "The Drone."

Also, I thank Ron Connolly for many years of valuable friendship. We have lived and survived together in Caesar's Gladiator Pit. To a great extent I look at my survival and intellectual development as being enhanced by your presence. A thousand questions and challenges you have given me. For twelve long years we have explored, debated, argued, and challenged the nature of things, both independently, and inter-dependently. You have given me a strong

CREDITS

example of loyalty and that characteristic is very seldom seen in its truest form. You gave me stability and the feeling of safety. Thank you, Ronnie, for being my friend.

Leroy Edney, I thank you for giving me the opportunity to look into the complexity, and humanity, of a young black man. Through your friendship, and others like you, I have been able to rise above some of my own culturally indoctrinated attitudes of misguided prejudice. And too, through our interaction, you have allowed me to help you rise above yours. Through our bond we both became wiser and stronger. Thank you, Leroy, for recognizing me as your brother.

Glenn Parks, I have watched you struggle over the many years against the social and interpersonal forces that would undermine me and my work. Because you are my boss in the institution's craft shop I am more vulnerable to you than to all others. Because of me I have watched you struggle with deep challenges to your authority, the system, your patience, and with your personal interpretations of man. Through your patience and your courage you allowed me the space, the time, and the opportunity to become a creative and positive human being. I have never lost sight of the fact that you have struggled to blanket me from some of the chaos of this environment. Thank you, Glenn, for giving me the time to study and prepare for a brighter future. You helped establish my link to the positive and productive side of man.

I would also like to thank Penn State

CREDITS

University for providing an educational program that brought a tremendous amount of human enlightenment into the dark shadows of these high prison walls. All of your teaching personnel were excellent in character and provided an example of the higher humanistic order in the nature of man. As a learning center for the people you have much in which you can be proud. Thank you Penn State for the renewed hope I found in your teachings.

Too, I thank all the educational personnel who have played a positive and significant role in the development of my life. Some of you have aggravated me into the dark depths of despair, and too, you have raised me onto heights that gave me vision beyond the normal perceptions of man. You have provided me with a sense of duty and now I will take what I have learned from you and attempt to pass it on.

Mr. V. Theodore Schreiber, thank you for the many years of encouragement and support for both my artistic and educational endeavors. You have been a strong advocate and a person I could believe in. Thank you, Mr. Schreiber, for having such a good human heart.

To my mom and dad I offer my deepest love and appreciation for bringing me into this life. Truly you handed me a tremendous struggle when I was born into such deep poverty. Somehow I've always faced the greatest tragedy, and calamity, during the evolution of my life. But in my youth you taught me to be strong. Without that

CREDITS

foundation I could never have been prepared to survive in this world in which I live. Through the life you gave me I've experienced the most intense and challenging structures that could befall any heart, or human spirit. The wonderment of it all has been a constant source of inspiration. Because of you, I'm determined to make my life purposeful and meaningful. I love you both very much, and too, I thank you for my brothers and sisters. You have made us all very strong and durable.

As for you, Beverly, I want to thank you for believing in me and for having the faith and courage to stand by me. Even in the face of adversity and uncertainty you remain loyal. For years you have struggled, daily, against the social tragedy that surrounds our love. You hug me when I paint my dreams. Ferociously you have guarded me, protected me, and given me a sense of love that assures my state of productivity.

When I look into the darkness of the uncertain future, your love and companionship provides a balance for me to lean against. You have taught me that man certaintly does need his woman. You have given me the courage necessary to venture out further into the darkness that surrounds us. You inspire me with a strong desire to build a future. You tell me to dare a real strong fight with Caesar. Thank you, Beverly, for loving me and for giving me a beautiful and firm purpose in my life.

As for you, Caesar, you are a thoroughly rotten son-of-a-bitch. I give to you that

CREDITS

which is due. You have treated me, and my people, as if we were less than human. You have stripped us, beat us, lied to us, isolated us, tormented us, and spit upon us. And, too, I have watched you rip and tear at all the good I have tried to build. You tell me it is wrong and against your law for me to achieve any meaningful social and personal accomplishments. I charge you with being counterproductive and working against the best interests of humanity. You try to represent us, as a people, as being evil. I say you are a liar, Caesar, and you are lost amid the depths of your own vindictive illusions. Add my book to your great and extensive library and we may all have a new sense of hope for our future.

Aubran W. Martin
Spring, 1985

DEDICATION

I dedicate this to you, God - to your flowers and to the greatness in your magic trees. I dedicate this to the peace you have shown me through vision, and to the mighty eruptions which echo from your holy sound. I dedicate this to the marvel of your greatest achievement - to the goodness that saves the world.

CONTENTS

1

THE PIT

Early I woke to the sound of loud screaming noise. The shadows in my prison cell were still darkly blended together as I felt the anguish of awareness creep slowly into my consciousness. I began to perceive complexities as I thought of my surroundings. I reached for a cigarette and coughed and choked as I lit it. "You're killing yourself," I thought as I pulled in another long puff.

I began to think of how to prepare for this new day. "It is no different from all the other days, months, and years," my mind responded. I raised up and clicked on the radio so I could distract myself with the sound of contemporary bullshit. It drowned out the sound of those early men who scream out their anguish so loudly. I looked up at the calendar. "Saturday." I took another puff of the cigarette and raised from my broken bed to make myself a cup of coffee.

I looked around my dark prison cell and thought of scrubbing out the dirt. Immediately my senses became alert as my eyes parked on the large envelope lying on the old wooden desk. "I received it from my friend, Ted, yesterday," I thought. I began to feel uneasy as I thought of the prison administrators holding it in their possession for three or four days before they gave it to me.

I sipped my coffee and stared at the envelope, trying to imagine the prison officials as they focused on the contents. "The bastards break every law," I thought, "and then they treat us like criminals." I frowned as I thought of their double standards, their lies and distorted perceptions. "Their structure is so illusionary and they communicate with a thousand tongues." I took another puff from the cigarette.

My mind contemplated the contents of the envelope. The thoughts frustrated me. Aggressively I grabbed the envelope, dumped out the contents and let them scatter across my bed. "Damn, I'm not a writer," I was thinking. I reached down and stirred my coffee which sat upon the ragged wooden chair. I angrily viewed the various documents as I thought of the frustration that came with them.

Contemptuously I reached down and tore my fingers through the pages and found poems I had written a hundred years ago. Too, I found short stories I never finished. "They were only experiments, things to pass time," I thought with belligerence. I sent them to Ted so he could gain a perspective of this reality. Now he sends them back and asks me to finish them.   "Dammit, I'm not a writer!" My mind screamed with protest.

"I don't like to write for long periods of time. I don't like forcing my mind to sit and squeeze out large organized and disciplined pictures of reality.   I don't mind keeping journals and writing small forms of observation, but I don't like to sit and squeeze out words that must be written over and over again." I thought of a million excuses as I pushed the work aside.

I reached down and snatched up the short story of "Caesar's Gladiator Pit."   Still, my mind resisted the thought of concentrating on it. I looked around for a distraction but there was none. "Ted wants me to finish it," I thought as I focused on the unfinished pages. I did not want to even read it.   "That perspective of reality is so dark, so challenging, forbidding, and frustrating," I thought.

I sat down on the bed, looked around my cell, and stared at the cross slats of cold-roll steel painted green to form my slave prison door. I reached over to the ragged wooden chair and grabbed the coffee so I could sip it. "You must do this, Buddy." My mind was now quite serious. I sat there and thought of descending into the depth of that complex dark pit again.

By this time most of the slaves were stirring from their darkened slumber. They began to scream out their rage and discontent. I sat there and listened to the insanity for awhile. I got up from the bed, walked to the sink and soaked two balls of cotton that lie there on the ledge. I stuffed them quite deeply into my ears. I packed them tightly so I could cut away the edge of their sharp protesting pitch. I stood there by the sink looking back across my broken bed. I viewed the scattered contents from Ted's envelope and I thought of how he wanted me to go back into the prison yard. He likes me to study the behavior of the men and their activity out there in that dark pit. I thought of how I disliked it out there. The thoughts made my mind scream and clash with conflict. It was like stepping through a magic door that hurls one back 2000 years in time to ancient Rome.

The thought of going into the pit again intimidated me. I walked back toward my bed and picked up the unfinished story. I fingered through the pages once more. "How can I avoid this work?" was a question that dominated my mind as I took another sip of coffee. I glanced around my cell and looked at the pictures that hung on the one hundred year old prison walls. Beverly, my woman, hung there smiling at me while looking out from under the frozen stress of well-hidden concern. She smiles and projects confidence as she hangs there, but I know my baby well. I can see the conflicting tensions stretched tightly across her brow . . . her eyes reflect the sorrow of pain. I glanced down to a ledge underneath my sink, looking for my armor.

"Damn you, Ted," I thought as I picked

up my sword. "And you, God, why am I forced to think like a warlord?" I removed the cotton from my ears but I heard no answer. I gathered my equipment to lay out the arrangement and check all the parts. I began to prepare for the dueling ritual as I stretched my muscles. I calculated my approach. I strapped on my gear and waited for the exercise bell. When the bell rang I waited for a few moments and then quickly stepped through the green slave prison door. I faced the fast moving faces of the on-rushing crowd. I stepped to the side of their stream. As they walked by I observed, and listened too. I listened to their language and I watched their expressions.

I caught bits and pieces of information that betrayed their character. One held a steel lock that was slid over his finger. He was telling his friends how he would crush the bones in the face of his enemy. They looked at him with deep admiration. Without them knowing it I measured both their strength and weakness. I filed away that treacherous look in my brain.

Too, as the men walked by I listened to them brag about the women they used to have and the possessions of their past life. They all had a song to sing along with the strings of their harp. Violence and intimidation were the major topics of conversation. Acutely I stood on the side, aware, watching them stream past me like dull-eyed cows in a herd. When the last one passed I fell in step at the rear. There I walked along thinking about

a poem one of the more perceptive gladiators
wrote. "Was it about a drone?" I wondered.

T H E   D R O N E
(In Memorial to D.L. Adamson)

What mighty tales those men would spin
from looms of broken dreams.
Pacing brick to brick and back,
and back again they came.

Their tales were hot-n-passion-filled
'bout harlots they had known,
ten-n-twenty dollar fucks
with girls who'd not yet grown.
Pacing brick to brick and back,
and back again they came.

Such tales of marks-n-scars they wore
told time-n-time again,
'bout how they'd pat you on the back
with bloodied hands and grin.
Pacing brick to brick and back,
and back again they came.

Some told of loves-n-lives they'd spent
and dues that had been paid.
Some told of lairs they'd hidden in
and times they'd got away.
Pacing brick to brick and back,
and back again they came.

They told of friends who never were
and ones who'd tried to be,
and Saviors who no longer saved
the likes of them-n-me.
Pacing brick to brick and back,
and back again they came.

The tales were mighty as the men
who'd boast-n-rant-n-rave,
but nary a man could spend the tale
to save him from the grave.

By Thomas G. Nickens

Down through the one hundred year old prison cell block corridor I walked. Foot by foot and step by step I came closer to the pit. I looked at the old and ragged windows as I passed them one by one. Each one was pouring in bright light. I watched the light bounce off the shadows it couldn't penetrate. "Damn," I thought, "damn" as I approached the big wide magic steel door that would hurl me back through time. I reached down and felt the razor sharp edge of my sword as I came closer to that dark arena door. I gritted my teeth and boldly passed through the magic.

Cautiously, on the other side, I stopped. And then into the gladiator's pit I walked as the stench of crowded and cagey living conditions infiltrated the nostrils of my mind. "Surrounded," I thought as I looked at the four

walls and at Caesar's sentry stationed on my
left. I looked around at the men who were
standing against the wall and were looking
for those who were weak and vulnerable. I
looked at them look at me. In another sweep
my eyes caught the men in the open arena
who stood in groups, in teams, that were
structured in various forms of association
which presented the dangerous daily rituals
of survival. "Gladiators," I thought.

About twenty feet just past the magic
door I stopped completely. I twisted my head
to feel the muscles in my neck. I then hunched
my shoulders to test the strength of my back.
Then I looked into my mind checking to see
if all the buckles were pulled tight. I tugged
at my defenses to see if they were snug and
secure. "I'm not ready," replied the insecurity
of my mind. I reached up to adjust the
sunglasses that were made like magic mirrors
and strapped across my face. They gave me
the ability to see out but no one could see
in. The magic of the mirrors gave me a
sharp edge. It forced the gladiators to look
at their own reflections and when they did
they became insecure. Too, I could observe
their behavior without letting them know they
were targeted with my calculation. And even
when I wasn't looking the magic mirrors made
them think I was. It made them move
nervously inside themselves. It made them
become like horses in their stalls when they
smell the smoke from the barn's fire. The
heat is not present but they know the fire
is near.

"BUDDY MARTIN"

By

Ron Connolly

I then touched the edge of my mind to feel the sharpness of my wit. My steps took me deeper into the mystery of Caesar's Gladiator Pit. The gladiators spoke to me as I passed them one by one. I acknowledged their greetings and spoke superficial kindness from great emotional distance. "One must be on guard," I thought to myself. I immediately thought of protection as the clanging of steel on steel sprang through the air and bounced off the hundred year old brick walls. "A man must be secure," I thought as my eyes searched out and measured the dirty colors that surrounded me and tinged Caesar's Gladiator Pit. My heart thumped a rhythm of discontent. I was now in the center of movement and my senses extended into crystal-clear awareness as I formed a region of safety. "Be in control of yourself," my mind whispered. "Hold a structure of discipline."

"Too much stress," I thought as I looked around for comfort. There was none to be found. I thought of my heart condition as I reached for a set of light weights to loosen up my tight muscles. "You must struggle," I said to myself with deep conviction. "You must prepare for reality." "I hate this shit," I thought as negative impulses dominated my thinking. My mental turbulance distracted me as I tried to concentrate on my workout. "Once again," I thought, "are you going to argue with yourself about the pros and cons of survival?" My emotional side raged with the demand for panic while my intellectual structures resisted. "Are we all for one," I asked, "or are we one for all?"

My mind began to compare the two world views. On one hand the theory is that man's nature is essentially selfish, greedy, and ruthless and that he needs law to guard and control him. They argue that without control man would destroy those who surround him in order to satisfy his selfish nature. I looked up and glanced at the gladiators who surrounded me. The other world view holds that man's nature is essentially kind and if left to his own devices he would be good and virtuous. They say if he could be left to himself he would build, develop, expand and care for all those who surround him. Again, I looked at the gladiators and glanced around Caesar's Gladiator Pit. "Are we all for one," I asked, "or are we one for all?" I looked at the armor and weaponry carried by the gladiators who surrounded me. I attempted to calm myself with intellectual puzzles. I had become good at the game of stress manipulation. I had to rationalize my position in life if I wished to retain my sanity and extend a positive destiny. "What was that question again?" I wondered.

On the weight pile I worked myself hard. There was a contest coming up. Man against man and strength against strength. Caesar, in the palace of his kingdom, had devised a set of games that would entertain his troops and the citizenship of Rome. In this region of his rule there were five major slave camps. Caesar, from his central office, enjoyed the game of manipulating camp against camp and slave against slave. There was something about watching them struggle as they attempted to destroy one another; it made the games so amusing. It made Caesar and the citizenship of Rom feel in control.

I thought about their delight as I worked my muscles. I knew I would not go to the games. I always embarrassed Caesar and so he kept me tucked away in the darkness of his shadow. I am viewed as a security risk and so he hides me and gags me so I can't make noise. I looked around and listened to the gladiator noise and wondered, "What makes me so different?"

"There is no way I can win," was the thought formed in the depths of my mind. "No one will hear your battle in the center of Caesar's dark and dreary gladiator pit." I thought about physical strength and I knew it was not my goal. But too, I knew I must remain strong. It was necessary for survival. "You must stay physically fit," I reminded myself. "You must be strong and mentally alert so you can map out your plans. Remember, you must survive. That is the path of life. You must go forward." Again, I looked around as I threw the light weights to the ground. "Man against man, or man for man?" I thought as I looked at the old rain and wind-worn wall. "I hate those damn one hundred-year-old bricks," I thought as I drifted into deeper feelings of emotional torment.

To my left worked a team of strong men. They were the strongest in the world of

Caesar's weight court. Not anyone in Rome, or among Caesar's guard, was as strong as they. From time to time they would growl in my direction, letting me know that I should push harder. "I know how to handle them," I thought. I asked if any of them would like a contest with me. I watched their gaze look blindly as if they never heard the sting of my words, but I viewed a smile edge up the corner of their lips. God, how I hoped they would never turn their strength against me. They were as strong as oxen on a busy day. I knew their growls were good intentions but their minds thought only of physical strength while my energy flowed in many directions. Confidently I picked up more weight. "I could go a hundred more, maybe," I thought. "But don't forget you have a bad heart." I cursed myself for that thought.

As I worked I knew when I thought of my heart condition I could not push as hard. "It is an unstable variable that must be processed accurately," came the reply of objective calculation. "Emotional input with negative probabilities should not be allowed expression." I thought about this type of discipline. "Which dominates which," I wondered, "the emotions or the intellect?" I resolved that the answer must be found in the structure of interacting combinations that exist in a particular location of time and space.

I looked around at the gladiators in my group. We were all strangers to one another even though we had worked together for a while. Communication barriers were up as we struggled to make conversation. We knew

full well that each was a potential enemy of
the other. Each studied and watched the other
silently. Each one gave fleeting glances of
observation as the other glanced back with
the same swiftness. Yet, we each encouraged
the other to push harder; to become more fit.
We needed each other but also feared the
potentiality we gave to one another.

"Push harder you lazy bastard," I said
with contempt to C. J. He buckled a bit under
the heavy weight but shifted his muscles like
clutches and pushed the bar up with power
to spare. As he raised his powerful body from
the weight rack he turned his gaze toward
me. With his eyes he told me I did not have
his physical strength and that he held that
perspective of glory. I knew he held me to
be contemptible but he treated me with
a quiet respect. He tended to test himself
by loud and aggressive projections of
intimidation. The rebound of his noise bounced
off the prison walls like a basketball. The
sound of his howl gave him confidence; it
verified that he was still alive.

I swung around to him sharply, looking
at him. My movements gave him a rush of
insecurity. I stopped short of him to pick
up weight and slide it on the bar. "Some
people have it and some people don't," I said
with a smile that disengaged his defensiveness.
His eyes became fleeting as he tried to figure
out if I had just complimented him, or knocked
him down. He did not have a strong sense
of emotional security and this gave me an edge,
a small edge, but it was an edge for my sword.
"Is he my brother?" I questioned myself as

I looked into the darkness behind his black mask.

"It's your down, strong man," I said real aggressively to a new gladiator. Rumor was that this slave was exceptionally strong before he was granted freedom by Caesar. But the wine, women, and the daily struggle to survive on his own had made him fat and lazy. Pudgy. He had run himself into the ground. But still he was already much stronger than I am, and larger. I could tell he feared strong and aggressive expression. I sensed this right away. He was not operating from a stable position.

The men around him were strangers and he attempted to jockey for power by projecting slow stubborness in movement. It was his turn to lift the weight and I watched the other gladiators move nervously as he stalled around in an attempt to command their attention. I gave it to him. "What's your weight?" I said with the sharp pitch of aggression. He attempted to look into my eyes to gaze at the spark of my intimidation but he encountered the reflection of my magic mirrors. Quickly his eyes darted to the ground. But then they sprang back to look at the structure of my physical frame. I observed him assess the limitations of my strength.

"What's your weight, brother?" Again I spoke with aggressive authority, but I accented the word "brother" with the echo of a slur. "You think you're smart, don't you?" he asked. His attempt to expand his security was obvious. My mind calculated his projections as I encountered the thrust of his aggression.

"It will take time," I said straight-faced and stern. "But we'll get used to one another." He told me he wanted 450 pounds. on the bar. "I want to see good disciplined lifts," I said as I added more weight to the bar. This time I spoke with encouragement.

The weight court at the edge of the pit had become one of my favorite places. It was tucked away in a corner. To my right was a high wire fence with round coils of razor-sharp barbed wire affixed to the top of the fence. On the other side of the fence was a small exercise yard used by the slaves that Caesar's men wanted to make suffer. I once observed a slave attempt to scale that razor-sharp wire. In the illusion that comes with panic he thought he saw the path of escape. I can still see him entangled and covered with blood in the shadows of my mind.

Behind my back is an old three-story brick cell block. The age old windows are barred and it is now used to store the gladiator exercise equipment. Rumor has it that because of the increase in Caesar's slave population the building will be used again for living. I once drew it with a magic pencil and to this day I still feel astonishment. The intensity of its inhumanity came through my fingers as it stimulated the nerves in my mind. The ugliness of its form and the texture of its character dragged across my heart like glass-studded sandpaper. There is a sense of evil there. I couldn't remember feeling the sense of such primitiveness before, not even when I was young and free and roamed through Caesar's slums. When the sentry saw the sketch he jumped on me and tore it from my grasp. He told me I was breaking Caesar's law.

To the front of me is a twenty-two foot, hundred-year-old rain and wind-worn brick wall. It is the bastard of humanity and reflects the nature of Caesar's spirit. The mortar between the bricks has patches that are different in color and in texture. Through the evolution of Caesar's reign new mixtures have been added to prevent the wall from falling down. The bricks are so aged that one can see canyons worn through their faces.

To my left is the main arena. It is the most treacherous part of the gladiator pit. Many games are seriously played there - to the death. Man in his most fearsome state and in his most deceitful illusionary acts carries out a drama of survival there. It is surrounded by the high old brick walls. And, too, there are plenty of seats for those who like to watch.

I wasn't particularly fond of the social dynamics that took place on the weight lifting court. However, the hard work distracted my mind from the darkness which surrounded me. One was constantly forced, through social interaction, to push further and try harder. One had to increase the amount of weight he could lift as the days passed into weeks. Slowly time progressed into months, years, and for some, decades. I constantly weighed the positive and negative aspects of this behavior. Truthfully, I did not like to lift weights. I had to force myself every day to come to the pit and activate this process.

"I have been lifting weights for about three years," I thought as I raised myself up from the weight lifting bench. I asked myself why I continued. Objectivity was swift with reply, "It enhances your probability of survival and serves as a stress relaxing buffer against anxiety-inducing agents." But I found conflict in that thought, too. I had the constant need to walk around and analyze the environment. This provided food for my spirit and I made sure there was no structure of interaction that my mind was not perceptive to.

However, if I decided not to lift for several days my body began to ache. I became ragged like the men who drank alcohol. I became irritated and found living inside myself difficult. I made a mental note to remind myself that if I ever wished to withdraw from exercise I should accomplish it through a slow step-by-step vanishing technique. Yet I thought of continuing because the rewards were positive. "A man needs positive rewards," I thought to myself.

I observed a strong gladiator attempting to bully the team into letting him lift lighter weight. "I'm the weakest man on this damn weight court," I laughed out loud, "but I can lift more than this lazy 'son-of-a-bitch' getting ready to get down." He whirled around and with his eyes threw hatchets into my heart. The entire weight court began to ridicule him with stabs of laughter. He jacked up his weight fifty more pounds. But then he turned and violently looked at me again. I felt a surge of insecurity shake my foundation but I never showed him that card. "Quit stalling, brother," I said aggressively. I stood there looking at him and thinking, "Sometimes a man needs negative rewards before he can achieve positive goals, but the dosage must be appropriately balanced with positive reinforcement." I stepped to him and patted him on the back. "You've been working hard today," I said with encouragement. "Don't stop now." He looked at me differently this time as he hit me lightly on my arm.

I grew tired of the weight lifting game as I gazed across the rest of the exercise pit. I looked for Ron and located him over on punk-iron row. "Punk-iron" was the name given to a section of the weight court where the gladiators are body building or just plain playing around with the weights. Often I tried to analyze how that section of the weight lifting pit got its name. I came to the conclusion it was because those men were not as strong as the more sincere lifters. I watched Ron struggle with the weights and I smiled deeply within myself. He was as thin as the height of a shadow as it lay upon the ground. But his thin frame made no difference when it came to combat. He was the most accomplished and seasoned fighter held in Caesar's Gladiator Pit. I thought of the ten years I had known him and the many challenges we both evolved through. He is my good friend and with concern I looked deep into the faces that surrounded him. "No danger," I said to myself.

"What do we all search for?" I asked myself. "Do we look for friends with the same intensity we look for enemies?" "You are searching for enemies," replied my mind. "You do not sit in a house of safety. You are not among friends and most of these men struggle in a constant battle deep inside themselves. You are in, and surrounded by, a state of desperation. You must evaluate these unstable variables continuously." I wondered about this and the thought gave way to leaving the weight court early. "I have trained enough today," I thought as I turned away and told the men on my team that I was finished for the day.

I knew what to expect as I walked away. I silently waited for the slings of ridicule as my gaze surveyed the surrounding environment. "There goes happy-do-little slipping away," came the attack. "No pain, no gain," came another arrow. I turned to look back as the entire weight court began to hurl vehemence at me. I smiled and waved good-by. I watched their body language as they kicked the dirt like disenchanted little boys. I laughed to myself, really it was a snicker, and I thought about defiance.

"Why does defiance make one feel so good?" I asked myself. "A man must be his own man," came the reply. "A man must establish his own goals and course of action if he wishes to find freedom and independence. He must make his own decisions and even have the strength to be the wind that blows in his sails if he wishes to actualize the greatness of his own potentiality. If not, he becomes a member of the herd." I thought of Neitzsche: Man becoming a dull-eyed cow and stepping into the shit that fell from those that led him.

I looked back at the fighters again and I thought of the injuries they gave to one another as they pushed each other to that higher mountain. "Is it man against man," I asked, "or man for man?" "No I will never be as physically strong as they," I thought. "But I will find my own path." I will climb my own mountains and I will lead the way. If I suffer injury it will come from misfortunes that befall the consequences of my own decisions. "I can live with the mistakes I make," I thought. "But I cannot live with the mistakes that come from following those whom I know are wrong. I will follow no herd unless that herd becomes stronger than me." I looked around at the herd that surrounded me. "Are they more powerful than I am, God?"

2

CRIME, PUNISHMENT, & PAST EVENTS

"Where is that damn outer perimeter?" I thought as I searched for the constant of the function. It determines the specific form of the process. If I could just find that determining factor, or characteristic, that makes up the form of this herd, I could then go to the edge and find freedom in the open plane. I began to think of the interpretation of freedom. How did the sage Rollo May describe it? "Freedom is in relationship to how man relates himself to himself during all of his moments." I thought about that. "He forgot about the environment," I argued. My mind was restless.

"I must be free," my emotions screamed. I looked deep into the well of my existence. I probed the core of my nature to find the disturbance. Down in the shadows deep within my being I found this little boy having an emotional tantrum. He was imprisoned inside a cold and love-empty steel cage. He raged and screamed and desperately tore at the steel bars. In panic he was out of control. He was blind to the barriers and rammed into the bars like a wild beast caught in the sharp jaws of a biting steel trap.

"Be careful," I said as my intelligence attempted to pamper him. "You're out of control and you will hurt yourself," I said in an attempt to sooth him with kind and compassionate words. He touched my hand through the bars and I felt his torment and sorrow flood through my heart. "It is my conviction to set you free," I said, "but you must be patient and work with me. The jaws of that trap are a complicated puzzle and if you pull too hard you will rip your own heart." "The lock on the jaws of that trap is controlled by three keys," I calmly told him. "Caesar and the citizenship of Rome have one, you have one, and so do I." I watched my child slide his key into one of the eyes in the lock. I slid mine into another. We both attempted to turn them together. "See," I said. "We need Caesar's key." Desperately my child looked at me. I slid him a set of bright watercolors through the cold steel bars and reminded him once more to be patient.

"Hello handsome legs. Did anyone ever tell you that you are the best looking man in here?" That sound brought me quickly back to consciousness. I looked to my right and saw a slender figure projecting a female form. Instantly my imagination transformed the

scraggly hair into a silky and shining afro.
My mind painted her eyes with the soft shadow
of blue-green. As she wet her lips with her
tongue my mind stretched bikini-like silk see-
through panties across her skinny ass. "That's
enough," I said sharply to myself as I realized
that she was a "hesheboy." "She's a man,"
I reminded myself. It was so easy to get lost
in this type of fantasy because Caesar and
the citizenship of Rome refused to let the
gladiators have human access to the love of
their women. "One must exercise a great
deal of discipline," I said to myself as I viewed
him acting and looking like he was pussy.
"She's a him," I said to myself as I corrected
the illusion, again.

Yet, I was tempted to play this distorted
social game. I remembered observing her down
on her knees blowing a gladiator in a far
corner of the pit where Caesar's sentries
couldn't see. I felt the surging power from
my loins begin to grow. "Well, I'll be damned,"
I spoke, "it's Hattie Maladie." "Is it true
that you are the kind of girl that will pour
water on a drowning man?" I asked. She sat
up straight and wrapped her arms around her
long slender legs. "Is this type of behavior
appropriate?" I wondered. I watched her
tilt her head back and show me her long and
tenderly sensuous neck. "Buddy, when are
you coming to visit me?" the hesheboy asked.
I smiled at the advance because in my need
I needed to be needed. Suddenly I felt
sensations coming from somewhere deep within
me. My consciousness was interrupted by the
thought, "You know better than this."

I glanced back at the hesheboy again, feeling the strong surge of power in my loins. "What is the feeling of your sunshine?" I asked. She eyed me with strong sexual hunger but as she spoke I heard a man speaking passion to me. "Are you insane?" I asked myself. I knew I was on unstable ground. I backed up a bit and looked at the illusions of the hesheboy. I began to prepare for departure. When I looked down I realized she had slithered her legs between mine to block my path. I swatted her on the ass with the flat side of my sword. "Good-bye young lady," I said to him with a smile. As I turned to leave I observed her eyes sparkle. He pulled up his long slender legs to let me pass.

"Will I always walk alone?" I wondered as I walked away. I thought of an old primitive poem I wrote years ago. I was young and tender then. My heart was still bleeding from the stab of losing my freedom and I was suffering deep pains of anguish. "What was that old poem my blood spilled out?"

WITH NO SNOW FALLING

1

It's Christmas Day
No snow is falling
I ask myself –
is this my calling?

To walk alone
in the prison yard tonight
Underneith the bright -
the harsh spot-light.

While families enjoy
each other's laughter -
The promises of love
forever after.

I ask myself -
is this my calling?
To walk alone
with no snow falling.

To enjoy no happiness -
through the cold night?
No Christmas tree -
with colorful light?
While families watch
their girls and boys -
Eyes full of glee
with brand new toys.

I ask myself -
is this my calling?
To ponder things -
with no snow falling?

To walk alone
in the prison yard tonight
Underneith the bright -
the harsh spot-light . . . .

WITH NO SNOW FALLING
2

I walked alone –
in the prison yard tonight
Underneath the bright –
the harsh spot-light.

My mind traced back –
to the precious years
When walking alone –
was not in my fears.

My wife and I –
walking hand in hand
Christmas shopping
in Santa's fantasy land.

I enjoyed her charms –
her precious laughter
She promised me love –
forever after.

To Christmas Day –
with beautiful snow falling
I lay in the bed –
My wife would be calling.

It is Christmas Day –
get up my sweet dear
My heart was happy –
with all of her cheer.

I was very heartbroken –
in the prison yard tonight
Walking underneath the bright –
the harsh spot-light.

I told myself, yes –
this is my calling
To walk alone –
with no snow falling . . . .

By Buddy Martin "72"

"Oh yes, I remember that old poem now," I thought. The ripples in the well of my memory began to make their associations. I looked into their reflections. I was in Caesar's dungeon then. The dungeon was housed inside a large penitentiary and they let me go outside to ponder. I walked alone in that small, brightly lit prison yard. My head was surrounded by razor-sharp barbed wire. The sentry on top of the wall shined his super-bright spotlight on me as I walked around in that little box. Forty-two days before I was condemned to die. Now I waited for them to come and hang me on that cross.

Slowly I worked my way back to consciousness; back to the gladiator pit. I became conscious of the external environment as I walked down the row of gladiators. They were sitting against the old brick wall. I noticed two of the sentries in my peripheral vision. They were watching me talk to Hattie

Maladie.   From a distance they snickered, discreetly they thought.   But the eyes behind my magic mirrors caught them when they thought I was no longer looking.

As I strolled past the sentries I didn't look at them but I watched them closely. They were looking off to my left with blank disinterested faces; but behind that mask they were watching me closely.   Quickly, I spun around and faced them.   "Gentlemen, how are you today?" I asked with a smile.   I watched their body language struggle with my stimulus. Their energy did not know how to travel as it surged into the extremities of their hands. I had made them slightly cringe.   I watched their weight shift as they spoke to me.   "Hi Buddy," they said.   Their eyes evaded my gaze.   They pulled their shields up around their chins like blankets.

"It could be worse," I reminded myself as I shifted my gaze.   I knew I was making Caesar's men feel uncomfortable.   From past experience I knew their instability could be dangerous and I felt my mind surge from the clashing images of past events.   I struggled against that feeling but the memories of past experience flooded me so quickly.   I was splashed with pain before I could sublimate my thoughts.

I could still feel their control sticks beating me.   The pain spread throughout my body.   Instinctively, I reached down and rubbed the back of my right leg.   I felt the deep indentation left in my muscle by the harshness of their crushing blows.   Too, I remembered the chemicals they sprayed on my body.   They burned big wide blisters across my chest and neck.   I could not remember seeing such high blisters before. The scent of the chemical made me sneeze and cry at the same time.

Again, I turned to look at Caesar's sentries. They triggered further thought as I remembered feeling the clamping bite of steel around my wrists and legs. Too, I felt the flood of humiliation as they chained me to the dungeon bars. I could still feel my feces and urine running down my legs. I felt the echo of their laughter burning its way through my heart as I kneeled before a toilet desperately drinking water from its contents. They refused to give me water for many days; but in my desperation to survive, I drank the toilet water anyway. "Look at him, he has lost his mind," I remember them saying. I looked at Caesar's sentries and remembered their voices and their laughter.

Before I realized it my mind pulled me back in time. I didn't like this memory trace and attempted to struggle against it but the emotional current was very strong. It took me back to when Caesar's men first arrested me and attempted to force me to make a confession for something I didn't do. Too, they wanted me to implicate a very powerful union leader in the crime. "Politics is so vicious," I thought as I drifted further back through that ugly memory. My vision was one of me on my hands and knees looking into that toilet.

Being forced to drink from a toilet taught me a great deal about myself. It also taught me about the nature of my keepers, and gave me insight into the social structure of the society in which I was raised. Constitutional safeguards as promised by our democracy were no more than sweet sounding words when compared with the reality of facing the bottom of that dirty toilet. "Where are my rights?" I wondered as I scooped up another handful of wet slimy vulgarity and drank it. In my desperate state I was shocked at how good and refreshing the water tasted.

I remembered turning around and looking at the guards. They laughed and ridiculed me. I reflected on a time when a fellow burglar who had served time told me when he was in prison some of the convicts washed their clothes in the toilet. I remembered scoffing at him. "There is no reality like that," I told him indignantly. Now here I was kneeling before a toilet, drinking.

What a strange and distorted world I was hurled into. Caesar's hunters arrested me along with two others. We were being investigated for three counts of murder. They imprisoned me inside a large stone fortress down on 21st Street. They locked me inside a double prison cell unit the guards called a "maxi-max." For months the county detectives, the state criminal investigative agencies, and Caesar's Bureau of Investigation waged a long terroristic campaign against me. They legitimized their behavior under the guise of "interrogation."

Caesar's Bureau of Investigation, the C.B.I., told me during the course of their many "interviews" they knew I did not assassinate the union boss and his wife and daughter. But they also made it clear that if I did not cooperate with them and name a particular union rival as the perpetrator of the crime, they would be forced to make my life very painful. They told me they completely controlled how I lived, or how I died.

Every time the C.B.I. approached me I told them I wanted my attorney to be present. They just scoffed at me. They told me over and over what they wanted me to say, and how to say it. When I refused they told me it was just a matter of time before I conformed to their wishes. They showed me a list of Congressmen and Senators. They told me to identify the names I heard the other two burglars mention. I told them I didn't understand what they were talking about. They again told me they knew I did not participate in the assassination, that I was deceived into thinking I was simply a driver and lookout for a burglary; but, if I did not make statements for them they would be forced to place the blame on me. I repeatedly told them I was innocent and if they knew I was innocent, "Why were they doing such a thing to me?" They remained silent.

They were particularly adamant about me implicating the union rival of the boss who was assassinated. They told me his name. They told me, "If you can remember the other two burglars mentioning his name we can make arrangements to charge you with a lesser crime, place you in an honor prison camp for a short period of time, and then arrange for your release." "We will

The Fortress On 21st Street

even supply you with a new identity," they told me. I was confused and did not know where that path would lead. They were extremely angry when I did not cooperate.

They told me one of the burglars who was with me was pointing the finger at me. They told me if I did not cooperate, I would be blamed for the assassination. Deep inside I was terrified. But on the streets I had learned that the cops always tell you that those who were with you have made statements against you so you will make a statement against them. I automatically assumed this was part of the process.

Too, I thought of when I was younger and incarcerated in reform school. I had observed the juvenile authorities manipulating the children in their custody. They always made promises that they would not keep. They would get the children to reveal information with phony promises and then kick them in the ass when they asked for payment. I thought of the articles I had been reading in the newspapers about the murder case. They were writing about a union and political assassination. I feared if I told the C.B.I. what I had learned someone may assassinate my family in an attempt to take vengeance against me.

The C.B.I. told me they would have me executed if I did not make the statements they wanted. It was crystal clear what they wanted me to do. They attempted to bribe me, intimidate me, and then they threatened to murder me. It was obvious they were attempting to structure a lie and they were

angry as hell that I refused to participate.
At that point it was hard to imagine just
how treacherous they could be.

"Such conniving minds," I thought as
I sat there looking into the eyes of the
C.B.I. men. I looked at their suits, their
shoes, and their clean shaven faces. I looked
at their neatly trimmed hair. I smelled
the air around them which was sweet with
the aroma of scented powder. "I always
thought they were good men," I remembered
thinking. Even when I was heavily into crime
I always held much respect for these men,
the elite of Caesar's Guard. But, now, there
I sat looking into the faces of criminals.
It was all very puzzling and baffling. I kept
looking at their business suits and thinking
about their police badges. I understood how
a street cop could be corrupt, but it confused
me to the depths of my soul to watch the
C.B.I. attempt to manufacture a lie. "What
the hell is going on here?" I wondered.
Quietly I watched them, waiting for their
next move.

"We have your brother locked in a cell
upstairs," one of the agents told me.
Immediately my senses sparked. My heart
pounded as it dumped adrenaline into my blood.
I tensed as I feared for my brother's safety.
Images of all the fights I fought in the slums
to protect my younger brother flashed through
my mind; I was on the edge of rage.

"It is up to you whether your brother
serves a long prison term or is released,"
they said. "We want the name of that union
official." One of them put his face close

to mine and said, "Make the statement and
we'll let your brother go home. If not,
we're going to crush his balls." "Whenever
you decide to set him free just send us a
note saying you are ready to make a
statement," they said. I looked at them all
dressed up in their beautiful suits as they
turned and walked away. In my heart I
saw my little brother crying in a dark
prison cell.

Who could imagine that those men, the
finest of Caesar's Guard, would manipulate
the law to make it look like a law was
broken, when, in actuality, they were the
ones breaking it. I sat in my cell and thought
of a news broadcast I once heard about a
fireman who secretly started a fire and then
doubled back to put it out. When caught,
they asked him why he did it. He told them
he wanted to be a hero. I sat there and
thought of the trap the C.B.I. set for my
brother.

They waited and waited for my note.
I wanted to write it but I didn't know where
such a lie would lead. Even though I was
confused and worried about my brother's
fate, I sensed it was better to not cooperate.
"My brother will just have to be strong," I
thought. But still, I remained tormented by
his situation.

My brother's only crime was that he
became involved in a family squabble with
my common-law wife. The C.B.I. used that
opportunity to manufacture criminal charges
against him. They puffed up charges against
him and then used that as a leverage to

force me into letting them use me. Since he knew the charges would not hold up in court, the federal prosecutor dropped all but one of the charges manufactured by the C.B.I. My brother was convicted of assaulting a federal officer. They convicted him for kicking one of them when he was arrested. They sent him to prison for five years. He forever carries the emotional scars of that experience.

When my attorney came to see me, with my seventh grade education I tried as best I could to describe what was taking place. My fragmented and emotionally charged words must have sounded like a little child trying to describe an experience beyond his ability to communicate. He looked at me in disbelief; I could tell he was bewildered. It was also obvious that he didn't believe me. He kept talking about wars between Democrats and Republicans. "What the hell is he talking about?" I thought. "What about me and my little brother?" I asked him. "Just remain quiet," he answered. I watched him in his nice suit, along with his shiny leather briefcase full of nothing as he walked away.

It was not long before the C.B.I. saw that manipulating my emotional bonds with my family was not going to work. They restructured their approach; they became more brutal.

One day the prison guards came to my cell and told me the C.B.I. wanted to see me again. I backed into a corner of my cell and refused to come out. "I want my

attorney," I told them. They left and came
back with more law enforcement personnel.
They opened the door and dragged me out
of the cell like an angry lynch mob. They
circled me and pushed me back and forth.
Then they started hitting me. I turned in
every direction as fast as I could, but as I
turned another one of them hit me. There
was no escape. They knocked me down onto
the cement floor and kicked me. To protect
myself I rolled up into a ball and put my
arms over my head. They used their riot
sticks to hit me across my ass and across
the back of my legs. One blow to the back
of my thigh severed my muscle. All I could
do was cry. When they finally stopped I
rolled over and remembered looking into
the face of a young officer who was about
my age. He spit into my blood.

This was when they shut the water off
in my cell. For three days I begged for
water, but they did nothing except insist that
I cooperate with the C.B.I. Instead, I kneeled
down and drank from the toilet. The guards
laughed at me, ridiculed me, and accused
me of being insane. In that moment I gained
deep insight into their world. There was some
sort of strange madness there. After they
had their fun one of them went and got me
a cup of water. As I drank, they watched
in silence. I sensed that they were not
finished with me yet.

Their next move was not long in coming.
They handcuffed me and left me in my cell.
After several days and nights my upper back
and shoulder muscles cramped and burned

with excruciating pain. I couldn't move; the pain was unbearable. I begged them to remove the handcuffs. They laughed. The C.B.I. agents came to my cell and told me all they needed was a signed statement implicating the union leader in the murders and they would remove the handcuffs. I screamed at them that I did not know a union boss. I told them that I had never heard of him. I watched as they walked away.

After suffering for several more days, I became desperate. I studied the handcuffs closely. In one of the youth slave camps I was trained as a machinist. As I studied the handcuffs I wondered what held them together. I recalled one part of my training that taught me about press fits - joints that when polished were invisible to the naked eye. I wondered if these cuffs were put together with press fits.

To test my theory I wedged the angle iron edge of my bed into the slot of the handcuffs. With as much pressure as possible I worked the cuffs back and forth, back and forth. The steel on the edge of the handcuffs tore into my skin; but that was not nearly as painful as the pain in my back and shoulders. I continued to apply pressure into the slots of the handcuffs until suddenly the pressure-fitted rivets snapped loose from the surface of the handcuffs. "These damn things are put together with press fits," I thought. And then with strength in my fingers I never knew I had, I ripped the cuffs from my bleeding wrists.

I immediately threw the cuffs in the

toilet and, for the first time in over a week, opened my arms and took on a more natural position. I was in ecstasy. God, what a joy that was. I felt as if a large thorn was just pulled from my heart. At that moment I understood why an animal caught in a steel trap would bite off his own leg to escape. I ripped and tore myself, but the greater pain was gone.

The guards were baffled when they found me sitting in the cell without the cuffs. They came into the cell and searched for the handcuffs. They fished them out of the toilet. The stainless steel that was once a pair of handcuffs now hung there all twisted, mangled, and broken apart. "How did you do that?" they asked. "With my will," I answered. They tore apart my cell as they looked for tools. I'll always remember the puzzled looks on their faces as they walked away.

Several times after that they again handcuffed me. Every time, when I was sure they were not looking, I snapped the cuffs from my hands. They had fits of frustration and rage. In one fit of madness they chained me to the steel bars by spreading my arms far apart. "Tear loose from that," they dared.

I hung there for eighteen days. They had me chained in a position where I could not stand up straight or sit down on the cement. I remember a black woman nurse came and rapped bandages around my wrists so the steel handcuffs would not dig into my skin and tear it so severely. She looked into my eyes real compassionately.   "That's the best I can do," she said as her eyes hugged me.

For eighteen days I hung on those bars. I defecated and urinated on myself day after day.   To feed me they took off one of the handcuffs and gave me a bowl to eat from. I was like an old dog chained behind the house that no one cared for. After several days in that position I didn't even care. At first there was a great deal of pain and I struggled to find some comfort. But after awhile everything became dull. Hanging there became my destiny. I no longer questioned it; it just was.

Lady Liberty

For years to come the C.B.I. and other authorities attempted to manipulate me through many forms of terror and intimidation. They then dragged me into court and convicted me of three murders I did not commit.   They sentenced me to die.   To them, justice was done.   Lady Liberty must have hung her head in shame that day.

After the jury sentenced me to die they returned me to my cell.   I stood at the toilet thinking of torture, the deals that were made, and the false testimony that was brought against me. I urinated blood as I thought of spending the rest of my life in Caesar's Gladiator Pit.

"Beware," came the voice of objective guidance. "Don't let that memory distort your perception of reality. They are not the same men." I looked carefully and deeply into the eyes of Caesar's sentries. They stood there nervously aware that I was contemplating them. I could tell they were puzzled by my gaze. I turned around and walked toward the corner of the cell block. From that vantage point I stopped and pretended to watch the slaves, but my gaze concentrated on Caesar's men.

I looked past their shields and through their armor, into their skin. I boosted the power of my penetrating gaze and went into their minds. "They are just men," I said to myself. "Some are good and some are bad." I stood there thinking about what they were thinking and I thought of how some of the good ones had treated me. Some of them were extremely kind and compassionate; they gave me water to drink when no one was looking. Some of them encouraged me to try and salvage my life. "Don't give up, Buddy," they would say. Others warned me when danger was near. At times, some of them gave me the opportunity to be human. But, too, there were those who were destructive and brutal. They would sneak in the night and deface my art. They would do all they could to ensure my personal failure.

Sometimes, when I walked past them, I could see the pain in their hearts. Each one of them had to struggle with his own conscience.

From my corner I imaginatively penetrated the minds of the sentries. I stared at their brains. I looked deep into their mental structures, deep into the pattern of their lives. I saw men engaged in a daily struggle for survival. I saw their anguish, their joys, and their fears. I saw their children and the worries that fathers have. I saw their wives and the bonds they shared. I saw their kindness and the treachery of their deceit. I looked at their armor, and they looked at mine. "Man for man," I asked God, "or man against man?"

I left the corner from where I stood and walked past the sentries again. I smiled at them as I walked by, but deep in my heart I felt a strong protest. It came from within the old, cold, steel cage my child was living in. I felt it rock and shake and I heard him kick the door. With a scream he shouted, "Bastards!"

The child in me did not like Caesar's men; not even the good ones. Once he was abused he did not forget, nor did he forgive. "Strange," I thought, as I looked deep inside of him, inside of me. I tried to look at him objectively and shrewdly. "What is your problem?" I asked. "Why can't you forgive?" The way he looked at me made me laugh; but, too, it made me cry. "They have me stuck in this trap!" he said emphatically.

"Well, young man, we have learned many

things from them," I reminded him.   "It has been through their brutality, their insensitivity, that made us both smart.   To escape the desperation from the infliction of their pain we have studied the known world and have discovered what lies beyond.   My child looked at me and spoke defiantly, "I want out of this damn trap!"

"That child in me," I thought absent-mindedly, "is a very difficult variable." "He is so tough to manage."   This thought seemed to ring a loud bell in my memory as I delved deeper into the swells of my mind. I stirred up those images and came upon a long forgotten past.   The feelings at that depth were so damn apprehensive.   I felt deeply frightened. I inquired further and from the darkness came a light that hypnotized me.   This time I was deep inside my spirit and looking through the eyes of my child.

"G r a n d m a ' s   H o u s e "

I stood outside my Grandmother's house on my tip-toes peeking through the window. I stood there apprehensively watching her stuff my ragged clothes into an old brown and wrinkled paper bag. She did not know I was secretly watching. "A bad sign," I thought. "This is truly a bad sign." Early the next morning I was up before the morning glory blooms. I sat on the porch swing along with the chilly morning dew watching for other bad signs. Soon they came in the form of a strange green vehicle. I sat there watching its weak shocks make it rock and bounce its way up the old twisting and dipping two-track dirt road. Immediately I darted from that old porch swing and ran to a flat rock at the end of the yard; there I stood like a billy goat waiting to greet the stranger. When he got out I was amazed. I had never seen one of them before. He was fat, black, and greasy, and he wore a shining blue suit. I backed up a bit.

Grandma came from the house with the stuffed brown and wrinkled paper bag. I backed up a bit more. She told me the nice man was from the welfare office and that I was to go with him. I didn't have to plan my escape - it was an immediate dash to the mountains. I climbed and climbed toward the top where the rocks became massive, and then I sat down on top of my world. From there I could see it all. Fifteen or twenty miles in every direction was within the scope of my vision. No hunter could sneak up on me.

I sat upon that mountain looking down

on the house below. I watched the old puffy-white smoke seep from that log cabin chimney and vanish into nothing. I looked at the old tin roof that lovingly sang me to sleep when it rained. I thought of how everyone became mad when I climbed on it; they said I would punch holes through it. "Grandma said her mom and dad built that house with an axe," I thought as I looked down at the strange vehicle, waiting for it to leave. I silently watched as the fat, black stranger drove back down the road.

I watched him go about three miles and then park under a tree. I sat there and shook my head. I was only six but that trick didn't fool me. I waited him out. About half an hour later I watched him drive back. He stayed about ten minutes and then he left.

I sat there watching him drive down the old dirt road for about five miles and then he turned onto the paved highway. He was heading toward Charleston. "Grandma said that's the state capitol and there they have a building with a dome made out of solid gold," I sat there and thought. I watched that green Chevy travel for miles; never for a second letting it escape my vision. Eventually it vanished among the hills. I spent the rest of that day parked on that high mountain perch watching and waiting for his return. But he never did.

In the evening I sat there and listened to the supper bell echo through the mountains. "Grandma was trying to trick me," I thought. It rang and it rang. I sat there and listened. It rang out the sound of a desperate cry.

I suspected Grandma was crying; but I sat there afraid to go home. I sat there deep into the night; afraid of the ˙dark, too. I could smell the snakes.

Finally, the hunger, the cold, and my fear drove me from my high mountain perch. I went to the house and, just as I had thought, found my Grandmother crying. I eased through the door. She was brushing her hair as she cried. Her long dark hair went all the way to the floor and I always found it to be so beautiful. "Grandma, was that a real nigger-man?" I asked. She pulled me in her arms and cried all over me. I cried, too. She told me that we were so poor and we hardly had anything to eat. She told me that she loved me but I was such a difficult child to manage. Such a difficult child to manage . . . such a difficult child to manage. "Such a difficult child in me," I thought, as the emotional waves in me drifted my consciousness back to Caesar's Gladiator Pit.

3

MY CHILD
AND
CREATIVITY

I looked around at the structure of the
sentries. Caesar had them disciplined to stand
in groups and never out of each others vision.
They were positioned in such a way that they
could see around every structure, and they
passed secret signals to one another; through
time I deciphered their signals and stole them
for myself. But now they had a new
technology. It was a little black box with
a red button on the side. They pushed in
the button and secretly whispered into it.
It made no difference, though, I still read
their thoughts by watching their focus of
attention and analyzing their body language.

I turned my gaze to sweep over the
gladiators in the pit. I looked down that
awfully long wind and rain-worn brick wall.
The gladiators sat along that long row of

endless pain and agony. I looked at the structure of their bodies, the design of their armor, and the shape of their shields. I pondered their weapons and the thrust of their treacherous deceit. "All to survive," I told myself. "God, are they my brothers?" I asked. Again, I pondered.

I attempted to analyze the internal structure of their minds. I felt my brain become stiff as if I were paralyzed. It made me think of gear wheels being jammed. "Their own energy working against their own energy," I thought. I pictured the image of clogged gear wheels silenced by confusion. "One wheel trying to go one way while another wheel tried to go in the opposite direction," I thought. "That machine will blow up," I concluded. Man should not work against himself, or against his brothers. "But, God, how can they be my brothers if they work so treacherously against me?" I stood there and wondered.

"Damnit, what a waste," I thought. I looked around at the activity and geared up my extrasensory perceptors. I penetrated deep into the shadows of the hidden part of the gladiator world. Discreetly I observed their secret movements. Immediately I caught the signals of their behavior and watched the intrigue. It was taking place both on my left and on my right. It was so subtle and yet so brutal; quietly there was a rape going on.

On my left a gladiator had his hand down the back of the pants of a hesheboy. His finger was stuck in his butt. I watched the pleasurable expressions on their faces; each one was trapped in the confusing state of deprived emotional passion. They were acting out the nature God gave their life in the vision of illusion - swearing it was real. On my right was a robbery. Several of the tougher gladiators were banded together and quietly robbing a weaker one, without violence. They did it through the cruelty of mental intimidation. I looked into the face of the weaker one and saw the shadows of terrifying fear; the tough ones were pouring illusions of monsters deep into the ignorant part of his brain. I reached down and felt the handle of my sword. "You are a non-participant observer," I reminded myself.

I looked further down to my left; the furthest point possible away from Caesar's sentries. "They are at it again," I thought as I watched some gladiators consume some magic smoke. It made the desperation of their pain go away. "I wonder why Caesar's men cannot see them?" I thought. But I knew the answer before the question was complete. We live in two different worlds. We can see them but they can't see us; and, too, they can see us when we can't see them.

As the gladiators got blasted on the magic smoke, it made them happy and talkative. They dropped all of their defenses; their protective shields clanged to the ground. I watched them throw away their swords and they danced with each other. Nervously, I glanced at Caesar's sentries. No one knew I was watching; they thought I was watching the hawk in the sky.

"Everyone thought they were so shrewd," I thought. The gladiators were getting stoned by the old stone wall and believing no one could see them. Caesar's men were making mental notes as they observed them while looking out at me. Everyone was operating under the impression that they were the only ones who could see. "Strange," I thought, "the silly games we play."

Caesar's men have the upper hand. They know how to play a real shrewd game. I thought about their strategy. Their game is to control the game, and they do a good job for Caesar. I watched the gladiators play with their magic smoke while Caesar's men wrote down their names. "They have a new technology," I thought. Caesar hired a band of wizards. The guards grab you and force you to piss in a bottle and then give it to the wizards to do what wizards do. If the wizards find smoke in the crystal glass, the sentries put you in the dungeon. But the gladiators, they are also shrewd.

Some of the more inventive, daring gladiators have a thin plastic bag of bright and clean gold piss. They tie it to a string and pull it tightly against their balls. When Caesar's men grab them to give them a wizard-test, they secretly pinch the skin of the plastic and pour the clean gold piss into the magic bottle. The gladiators pay other gladiators that are smoke-free a carton of cigarettes for their urine sample. I stood there and wondered what the wizards thought when the piss was two months old.

I wondered about the complexities of

the pit and I began to find it difficult
managing all the structures in my mind.
Immediately I was diverted to a stressful
tension in my body. My muscles were as
tight as the tension in a tightly strung bow
pulled all the way back. "Relax," I told
myself. "Manipulate this." I took ten slow,
deep breaths and concentrated on relaxing
my muscles. As I stood there I withdrew
into a deep state of meditation. I pulled
darkness deep inside myself and sat down
in a room where there was no sound except
for the running and babbling brook. I quietly
listened to God's nature. But through it all
I didn't close my eyes.

Quickly my intuition instructed me
to duck. Unconsciously I watched the faces
around me and I noticed they were
concentrating on a fast moving object in the
sky. They began to scatter like the wind
on the tip of an arrow as it aggressively flies
at its target. Behind me a ball smashed
against the wall. I cursed silently, but
endlessly. "There is nowhere to relax," I
thought. I looked around, seeking a
peaceful shelter. There was none. "Ducking
from that damn ball is a constant variable,"
I told myself with a great deal of silent rage.
"You must adapt," came the reply of logic.
"Fuck you!" my emotions screamed out. I
turned around to look hatefully at the
gladiators playing with that ball. "They need
something to occupy their minds so they can
retain their sanity," I said to myself, "even
if it is only a ball." With that thought I
began to calm myself down.

I looked around at this crazy-assed arena. I looked for someone who I could have a reasonable conversation with. There was no one to be found. I looked down at the dusty old dirt and then I stretched my gaze to create a wider vision. There was not a blade of grass to be found. There was nothing to associate with God's nature other than the trampled earth I stood on. A vision of a tree entered my consciousness. I looked down again at the dust and the dirt. I began to think of death. "What was that old poem I wrote a hundred years ago? Did I write that in the year of seventy-two?"

If I remember correctly, it was in autumn when the poetic beauty and sadness of being deprived from God's nature inspired me. I was walking alone in one of the smaller asphalt-covered arena yards when I noticed a leaf riding and sliding across the wind. Over the old rain and wind-worn wall it came. It was a chilly wind that carried it. Before it left, it whispered in my ear that snow would soon begin to fall. It had been several years, then, since I had seen a leaf. When it skidded to a halt on the hard asphalt like a child's paper plane, I was pulled to it by the magic. Tenderly, I picked up that welcomed wonderment and pondered its being. I thought I saw its tears and felt its fears of dying in a strange land. I stood there and thought about its life fading from the crisp structure of its lonely beauty. In that moment I couldn't control the feelings of my own life slipping away. Too, I was a stranger in this strange land. "What did my magic pencil say?   What were those soft and bitter words?"

A   L O N E L Y   D Y I N G   L E A F

Tenderly . . .
The early morning twilight of autumn –
kissed the summer breeze farewell
Bringing to the prison slave-yard
a lonely dying leaf . . . .

The leaf is dead –
its past is gone
The tenderness –
will not go on
Throughout its life –
there was a place
But in this prison slave-yard
it died with grace . . . .

By Buddy Martin "72"

        The day was yet young.   I had the rest of   the   afternoon   and   evening   to   contend with before I could lay down to dream my peaceful dreams.   I needed a place to sit. I drifted toward the open spaces in the gladiator pit.   Most of the gladiators avoided this   section.   They   feared   open   spaces. I looked around at them and most were up against   some   part   of   the   old   brick   wall.

Some were walking here and there. They seemed to be walking everywhere, but I knew they were going nowhere. I sat down in the open space right in the center of the dusty old dirt.

I looked up at those walking by looking at me. The expressions on their faces told me I aggravated them by sitting where I sat. I was in the middle of everyone's path, but I stayed there anyway. I watched them walk in front of me, behind me, and to both sides of me. I looked up at them from a dog's-eye view. "Why do some artists have such a strong need to express this perspective?" I wondered. My mind turned to art and immediately my imagination shifted gears.

I watched the wheels spin and complimented myself with logical comfort. "You have a finely tuned machine. God gave you a good one," I thought. My mind's eye raced here and there looking at my powerful structure. I could hear it hum, somewhat, in a resting state. I looked down deep into my child in the cold and bare steel-barred cage. He was now alive with attention and his eyes glowed firey creative sparks of anticipation. "You must set me free," he said. Again I listened to the resting power of my creative machine. I sat there and wondered about the magnificence of creativity. Everything in me became still with awe. I felt that my machine wanted to surge; to blow the dust from the powerful channels of expression.

Fast moving action in the pit broke my

concentration and immediately I was on my feet, gearing up for action while acute perceptions analyzed the surrounding environment. "Just one of them chasing that damn ball," I thought as I sat back down. It was the weekend and I disliked this time of the week tremendously. It bored me, and I was unable to get access to materials I needed for free creative exploration and expression. This part of the pit was not suitable because it was highly charged with intimidating social variables. This kept one locked into a frenzy that established harsh boundaries of defensiveness; boundaries which are contrary to the best interests of creativity.

"Can I rev up the engine?" I heard my child ask from down deep in his cold bare cage. "He wants to be creative all the time," I said to myself. I sat there looking deep within myself, inside of him. He was always plowing some sort of ground; always tilling the soil. He liked to turn over everything, flipping it over and over and over again as he inspected it. He liked to look into all the cracks and crevices, and he would go back time and time again just to make sure he never missed anything. He would stab his finger into the darkness of the unknown to look around. Yet, too, he was smart; he knew when things were not right. He was very sensitive. He left it up to me to keep him alive. He always told me that I had to explore everything time and time again so I would know it well. He kept me alive.

Deeper I looked into him by looking

into me. I began to reflect on my art and how that child in me affected my work. "He is my beacon," I thought. The grownup in me follows him; and when I don't I lose my way. Again I looked at my creative engine. It was, at the moment, power in a resting state and by its nature it had the need to be set free. I could hear its racket rocking, and from that sound I knew the machine was tightly synchronized. "Strength," I thought.

Damn, creation surely amazes me. Again I looked at my child. I could feel his rhythm in the beat of my heart and my soul knew he was alive. "He is my spirit," I thought. I could feel his quiet rhythm churning and I knew his power branched into eternity. His branches are so abstract I cannot completely trace them with my objective consciousness. He is so complex that he is a damn difficult child. What is it about creativity that makes him so alive? I looked at him laying there in his cold steel cage. I knew he held the secret to many wonderful things. But he is so stubborn and he cannot explain things to me easily. "And even now," I thought, "he lays there listening to my thoughts."

I sat there and thought about my art and how I followed my child. "What is the secret of our partnership?" I wondered. "How do we work so well together?" I thought of how I let him lead, let him explore, set him free and then follow the trail he paves. "The damn fast-moving little bastard leaves me all kinds of crazy messages in the wake of his path," I thought.   He leaves it up to me to make sense of them.   Sometimes I can and sometimes I can't.   Sometimes I can figure them out easily and quickly, but sometimes it takes me years.   Sometimes he leaves me mind-twisting puzzles that get me lost amid his creative sea.   He doesn't even slow down when I begin to stumble. The only way I can stop him is if I grab him, and then he tries to bite me.   I looked down at him in his cage and I laughed.   I laughed deeply; and I heard him laugh, too.

"He has taught me so much," I thought. I watched him closely.   He runs to the far-reaching edges of the universe, scoops up the elements, and throws them like dice; leaving me to unravel their patterns.   Too, he talks straight to God.   They have a real strange language.   When he talks to God I have to be silent; I have to even stop thinking.   I have to sit on the side and watch while God tells him about the masterplan.   They are such deep and far-reaching visions, such an incredible state of beauty.   When he and God talk, I can see such clear visions in my mind. They are more pure than what man can see with his eyes.   God talks about law.   When I marvel at the visions I am truly hypnotized. They are laws I don't think I can pass on to others.   They are so complex and sophisticated.   I believe they are private secrets that will forever stay in my nature.

I thought about my child and how he likes to gamble; he goes into all the dark spaces.   I could feel a ripple in my mind and its surge pulled me down into the depth of passed time. Again I looked through the eyes of my child. When young I always ran to the door and opened it at the sound of any knock. I was curious like that. My mother would always scream with apprehension when I did. We were new in Rome and she kept saying that the boogie-man might be out there. I would run and open the door anyway; until one night I was shot.

A knock banged on the door just after it turned dark. I ran to the door and pulled it wide open. A young nigger-boy stuck his gun in my face and pulled the trigger. The sound exploded in my ears like the shot was inside my head. The flames boiling out of the barrel raced toward my face faster than the snakes that used to try and bite me. I fell over backwards, both hands pulled up against my face. I began to have spasms and convulsions along with my screams. My mother desperately tried to pull my hands from my face and I heard her praying, "Oh, my God." Fortunately the gun was only a blank. She slowly loved me back to a state of calmness. But that child hid in me. I couldn't find him for years. There was no more play.

I surfaced to consciousness; back where I could look at my child. He had been lying there dreaming of past things. "He has no fear," I thought to myself. And me, I look at myself as timid. What a strange combination. "Each one enhancing the other," objectivity said. You protect him with your defensive inhibitions and he frees you from your fear. "That makes a good balance," I thought.

"But he makes me so damn apprehensive," I thought. "He climbs, tears, rips, gouges, cuts, puts things together that don't belong together, and he goes through everything like a young primitive whirl-wind. He ties, binds, glues, stacks, nails, stretches, saws, bends, warps, distorts, and pisses on things." I sat there thinking about the time he built a sculpture in the dungeon out of styrofoam cups. He used my cigarette as a welding rod to fuse the cups together. He drew on it with black ink; that was all there was. And then he stood up and pissed all over it to create new colors. I stood there amazed when the pink, yellow, and blue crystalized. Somehow he made red and blue violet appear with the magic of his piss.

Riddle of the Sphinx

Caesar's bureaucrats went wild when they saw that sculpture emerge from the darkness of their dungeon. One of them went into a rage and threatened to smash the sculpture to bits. Another screamed, "This is against the rules!" The very thought of building something productive and of value in the depths of Caesar's dungeon created dissonance in their minds. For them this was an intolerable situation. I watched as their faces expressed a high degree of incongruity and disbelief. "That damn child gets me into so much trouble," I thought.

As I reflected further on the guard's bewilderment I laughed out loud. With that I became conscious of the fact that I sat in the dirt by myself. Immediately I looked around to see if anyone was looking at me. Caesar's sentries were, and I worried that they would think I was crazy. "You cowardly bastard; you are afraid of your own emotional shadow," my child said. I sat there and thought about that. I looked at him lovingly. "Do you know that the hands of the Creator gifted you?" I asked. "I am the hands of the Creator," he said. I sat there and looked at him. "He teaches me so much," I thought.

I remembered watching him constantly work the creative machine. "I am a scientist," I said to myself, "and I study by letting my child work that machine." When he manipulates the wheels and pushes the buttons, he turns my world into a strange magic ride. Admittedly, I become apprehensive as I watch him manipulate the mechanisms of my mind. "Does he know what he's doing?" I asked myself. He pushes in the clutch and he shifts the gears back and forth so quickly. He revs up the engine and makes the wheels spin. Even when I'm not working with my art he creatively spins my wheels. I guess he does that just to ensure the wheels work adequately and to feel the thrill in the surge of his power. His movements synchronize with the racket-rocking of my creative motor and he projects a great deal of confidence.

I looked at him down deep inside the spirit of me. I wondered why he seemed to know how everything worked. "This is my house," he quietly told me. As he spoke he never stopped to watch what he was doing. "Don't mess anything up," I said back to him with harsh criticism. "Watch what you're doing." He laughed at me and I could feel his laughter bubble up from the depths of my mind. His happiness filled me and I laughed back with him. I looked at him closely because I knew he would tell me many puzzling things. Many times they were difficult to catch, like a curve ball.

My mind reviewed the many years of art my child produced. I gazed over the sculptures, drawings, watercolors, and paintings, and how he sculpted three-dimensional arrangement over the paintings and then painted on top of the sculptured arrangements. He would hand them to me and say, "Analyze." I would then write technical papers. His message was always so damn complex. One day, after he had been communicating with God, he told me he knew how the universe worked. "I'll bet you do," I said. He laid down and cried out a rage because I didn't take him seriously. Finally, after about five years of listening to him, I now take him quite seriously.

I tried to look at him real objectively as he played with the creative machine. But he would flood me with so much information that he would out-produce my capacity to logically analyze. "When you are shifting the gears and pretending you are going everywhere, but going nowhere, what are you looking for?" I asked him. "I'm testing," he said, "the safety of the functioning process." I thought about this for a moment. "How can you tell if the creative process is unsafe?" I asked. "When I'm shifting gears, it is in my wrist," the child said. "It's an intuitive process." "And what is the intuitive process?" I asked. "Sensitivity," he answered. He went on to explain that when things are amiss he would intuitively know through his degree of sensitivity, and from that he would know it was not the proper time to accelerate the creative machine. "When things are amiss, what do you do then?" I asked him, watching shrewdly. "I tell you to look in your logic smart-bag and fix it," he said. "And how do I fix it?" I asked. "You remove me to a place of safety," came his reply. "He sure is confusing," I thought to myself as I quickly flew back to the reality of Caesar's pit. Intuitively sensing something was amiss I put my child away in a safe place.

4

THE SCRUFFY GLADIATOR

Something in the social environment was out of the ordinary. It was a gladiator buried among the movement of some other slave men. He was moving behind them, but he was focused on me. I let my eyes sweep past his vision as if I were unperceptive to the direction of his focus. I knew a sharp penetrating look from me would intimidate him and he would shy away. I was purposefully looking in the opposite direction when he came upon me. He stood over me feeling a strong sense of security. I reinforced his stance even more by pretending to be startled by his presence.

Behind my magic mirrors I analyzed his projections. His armor was scruffy, shoes battered, eyes were dull, face rough with uncaring care, eyebrows were heavy, his body was sloppy, and his hair went here and there. I already knew what he wanted, a cigarette. But I acted disoriented when he spoke. "Do you believe in blue sky and night thunder?" he asked. "Most all of the gladiators swear he's insane," I thought. I sat there and looked up at him thinking, "Boy, you don't know what you're getting yourself into by trying to play crazy games with my child. He loves to play and he'll run you ragged."

Intently my child processed every variable, but he pretended to be confused. I was sitting but I decided to lay way back and grind myself deep into the dusty old dirt. I looked up at the sky and I stretched my body until all the tension was gone. I shifted my magic mirrors so he could get a better look at his power. I watched him try to look at me but all he could see was himself. I then flashed the sun in his eyes just to intimidate him a bit. He became confused.

I shifted my mirrors again; I didn't want to scare him away. "Would you like a cigarette?" I asked. He shifted his weight and smiled. The dullness in his eyes faded as I handed him a smoke. "What have you been up to?" I asked. I watched him look around and I could clearly see torment reflect upon his face. I shifted my mirrors so he could not see his own reflection. Again I reflected sunshine into his face; it was a hypnotic glitter that pulled him closer to me. "Sometimes it is difficult for a man to look at himself," I reminded myself.

As I observed him I felt the uneasiness in him become uneasiness in me. "This is only transference," came the note of psychiatric objectivity. "Go forth and him out." I looked at him closely as I went past his superficial surface and into the internal makeup of his mind. "Why do you

pretend you're insane?" I heard my child ask.
The scruffy gladiator immediately sensed that
there was no avenue of escape. My child's
question had him surrounded. He looked at
me more closely and discovered the magic
mirrors that were flashing in his eyes. "He's
becoming more perceptive," I told myself.
"He's beginning to analyze." I reached up
and pulled down my mask of mirrors. As
I took off my glasses he smiled a deep trusting
smile. "Would you like to sit down?" I asked.
He looked at me and laughed. "In the middle
of everyone's path?" he asked with a look
of disbelief. "Won't they think we're crazy?"
"I suppose," I said as I looked around at the
confusion in Caesar's pit. "But can you find
a less crowded space?" I asked. He glanced
around the pit and sat down to my left.

I let him rest for a moment as he
looked at me from a safe distance. My child
was impatient, again he advanced with the
sting of his magic prod. "Why do you act
like you're crazy?" he asked. I already knew
the answer but I wanted the scruffy gladiator
to tell me himself. He looked at me from
underneath his lowered brows. "People avoid
me when they think I'm nuts," he countered.
I sat there piecing the structure of my next
words together carefully. "This place really
frightens me," I said. As I spoke I looked
away from him. I didn't want him to know
that I could see his fear, too. He gave no
response. I turned my gaze toward him quickly
and squarely. "Can you see fear in my eyes?"
I asked him. His gaze darted to the ground
to evade my aggressive confrontation. Once

again my child rushed him with the sting of
his prod. "Are you afraid of people?" he
asked with a sting. "I'm not afraid of
anything," he lied as he mustered the courage
to look defiantly into my eyes. I turned my
gaze away so he could regain a feeling of
security.

"Many people are afraid and don't
recognize it," I said. "Only a man who is
unaware of the treacherous reality in Caesar's
Gladiator Pit is without fear. Are you
insensitive to this environment? Are you
really crazy?" I asked as I looked deep into
his being. He began to loosen up. "Do you
think everyone is afraid?" he asked as he
looked around at the fear in Caesar's
Gladiator Pit. With that I began to drift
in thought. I dove deep into my own past
and personal world. I looked at the day
Caesar's sentries brought me here - a hundred
years ago. I had been raised as a pagan
barbarian and my tribe dwelled in the
Appalachian Mountains; digging coal from those
black hills. We were a poor people. The
desperation of hunger drove us from our
land. We migrated into a large city called
Rome.

I remembered well the Roman slums.
The people were so odd and different. The
children would jump on me and whip me when
I came from our hut. I couldn't understand
their language. They took my possessions
and beat me because of the way I looked
and talked. I tried to fight back but they
formed gangs and beat me even worse. And
when I cried it made no difference. "I have

always lived in fear," I thought to myself.

There was no alternative back then except through violence. I remembered the day I looked out of our window and saw two of the leaders; they were twins. I rushed from our hut enraged and full of vengeance. I bit them, scratched them, gouged them, and clawed at their eyes. I hit them, kicked them, stomped them, and threw them in the thorns. From then on I was one of the guys.

They taught me how to hustle the citizens of Rome. We would shine their shoes and pick their pockets. We would snatch their pocketbooks and run through the back alleys. We would leave them to scream out their rage as we passed. And the elderly, we would get them too. We would knock on their doors with young innocent faces asking if they would like us to go to the store for them for the fee of a quarter. When they gave us their money we would run to Caesar's carnival and ride the big wheel with a snicker. We left the elderly feeling empty.

And, too, as I grew older the game became more vicious. We would gang up in a wolf-pack and seek out a feeble lamb. He would be drunk and singing; he made it easy for us. We would tear away what resources he had. In our wake he would lay there mumbling to himself, bleeding. And, too, we would steal the Roman chariots and take them for long, wild rides. I would have a hundred horses under that hood and with the sting of my whip I could make them all run. There were all kinds of buttons, all kinds of levers, big leather-covered seats, and magic music coming out of the dash. We would screech and holler and laugh, never realizing we came closer to our graves. Mother and Dad were always saying I was with the wrong crowd. But what did they know? There was no other crowd.

Caesar's men chased us as we ran about his town. We tore up the roses and threw apples at his clowns. We went into those bright, shining stores and stuffed our pockets with candy and rings. We stole everything. Everything was rip and tear. We knew no other way. One by one the children fell and Caesar's men grabbed them with a tight grip. From time to time they grabbed me, too, and beat me with their whips. I would rant and rave and they would whip me some more, taking from me what I had stolen. I watched them laugh at me as they divided up the stolen property; they stuck it in their pockets. They would not arrest me because if they did they couldn't keep it for themselves. When they were done they kicked me in my butt and threw me from their black and white chariot. I dusted myself off, licked my wounds, and then looked for something else to steal.

Eventually the game became more brutal and I was sent to the slave camp for the young. There I learned about real treachery, and the game changed again. I watched them rape each other and walk away with smiles. I looked at their victims lying bleeding and fucked upon the ground. Once I watched ten boys take their turn; I counted them one

by one. They turned to me and asked if I
would like some fun. I looked at their victim.
"One of their own," I thought. At that
point, I backed up. It was then that I made
a hatchet.

The youth slave camps hardened and
calloused me. They inflicted pain and
anguish deep into my spirit. They brought
into sharp focus the darkest side of humanity.

In Caesar's youth slave camps the
children were like savages. I watched them
rape and brutalize one another. One would
climb on top and begin to grind on the lower
one and then another one would pile on top
of him, and so on and so on, until there was
a stack of them all piled up and grinding
away on each other's asses. The guards would
sit there laughing and pointing. All normal
contact with the outside world was lost;
culture shock was an everyday event. Even
though I was street-wise and a tough ghetto
child, I was not prepared for this. Emotional
and mental turbulence became my constant
companion.

I watched them rape, and then fight
to stop from being raped. The strong were
brutal. The weak were treacherous and
cunning. And then, from time to time, when
they made me their target, I too became
vicious. Young boys in their desperate
struggle to survive taught me how to live in
Caesar's Hell.

I looked into their mouths; the broken-
off teeth and hairline cracks told me of
their combat. Their knuckles had jagged and
brutal rips from the many crushing blows.

Their eye sockets were scarred. In Caesar's youth camps violence was the norm. As time went by, I too became violent. This is when they started to let me alone.

I watched those who attempted to be passive; to survive by not fighting back. At first it was only the tough ones who fucked them. But, as time went by, the weaker and cowardly ones creeped forward to take their turn. And then, as if to secure their place in the dominance hierarchy, those who were abused became the abusers. The strong dominated the weak, and the weak banded together to abuse those who were still weaker. In time the pecking order was clearly established. For months I silently watched the primitive Darwinian ritual.

I especially remember one young boy who was at the bottom of the hierarchy. He was terrified by violence; he was abused by them all. His gentle spirit was ripped and clawed until all human dignity was lost. I watched him become silent and withdrawn.

What could have been his tormented state of mind when he taped those razor blades between his fingers? What was he thinking when he ran screaming like a wild beast into the early morning showers? He cut and clawed his way through those who had abused him. He cut their naked balls. He tore at their jugular veins. They all fought and struggled to get through the shower door at the same time. Many did not make it in time.

I was in the rest room when I heard the screams. I stepped into the shower room

and caught the end of the frenzy. Blood was
dripping from the shatter-proof stainless steel
mirrors. It was splattered on the ceiling from
the slinging momentum of desperate movement,
and smeared thick like grease on the shower
walls. I looked at the young dude who before
wouldn't fight back. He stood under the
shower laughing and rinsing away the blood.
He then walked over and tore the taped
razor blades from his fingers and one by one
threw them into the industrial sink. When
they shipped him from the institution some
of the personnel said he was insane - that
he needed treatment.

From it all there was trauma in my
soul. Deep inside the chambers of my mind
remained frozen a howling jagged and
shattered scream. The internal turbulence
of my spirit clashed and tore at the
boundaries of madness as it attempted to
destroy me. I was alone and adrift upon
the churning waves of a violent sea; a world
I had never known or even imagined engulfed
me. After Caesar's juvenile reform school
life was no longer a game filled with fun
and challenge; now it was a matter of life
and death. Back then I sat with darkness
and confusion as my companion and guide.
That was the only way I knew. The only
way I had.

From the youth slave camps I escaped
one by one. I never really knew where I was
going but I knew I didn't belong there.
Slowly the years passed and they transferred
me from zoo to zoo. I was getting older
with a desperate wisdom as my life grew

dim. I was getting closer to a darkness that this world would show me. Someday I would be in Caesar's Gladiator Pit.

"Hey," I heard the scraggy gladiator say, and with that stimulus I surfaced back into the reality of Caesar's pit. "Are you sure you're not crazy?" he asked. "What makes you ask that?" I retorted as I focused on his scruffy face. "When I talk to you, you disappear," he said to me. "Where do you go?" I smiled at him. "I'm a dreaming traveler," I said as I looked deep into the blue sky and thought about thunder. "Do you think we're all afraid?" he asked me again. I dove deep into the swells of my memory to look at history. Caesar hung me on a cross and sentenced me to die. The Roman citizens cheered and laughed and gave me thumbs-down. They wrote my name everywhere. They said I was the most evil man, and they left me to hang by myself. I hung there five years waiting to die but that day never came. To pass time I lived in the past. And, too, I dreamed. Then one day they came and cut me down and threw me in this pit. For a while, so I wouldn't lose my mind, I wrote some poems. "What was that poem I wrote a hundred years ago?"

I AM AFRAID

Though it can't be death -
that I'm afraid
For I am dead of living -
dead of dying

Dead-buried-no flowers
I am afraid –
afraid of living
Forever in this coffin . . . .

By Buddy Martin "72"

I looked at the scruffy gladiator. "I am deeply frightened," he said. I quietly sat there and looked at his fears. He was lost and disoriented and I knew he was close to tears. I felt the child in me become disturbed. My own emotions were near. I reached over and touched him on the shoulder to brush away his fear. "Man for man," I asked myself, "or man against man?" The gladiator raised his heavy young head and looked at me somewhat calmer than before. I could tell he was relaxing as he stretched out his legs. "How do you deal with the treacherous ones?" he asked as he leaned back on his hands and stretched out his chest. I gazed around the pit watching the gladiators and thinking about past combat. I watched them whisper to one another and thought of conspiracy. Each one was trying to find weakness in the next; and, too, they were bonding together for cooperative hunts. "How do I handle the treacherous ones?" I asked myself. I began to think of them; the ones who cut your throat and then spit in your blood. "How many have I known?" I quietly asked myself. "How many have tried to destroy me, or conspired to do so?" I began to think of their schemes.

"What is it in a man's blood that drives him to kill?" I wondered. I looked around at the swords and other weapons of the gladiator trade as they practiced in Caesar's pit. Some sat there sharpening the edges and filing the points. I watched them devise their gimmicks and practice illusive tricks. Some were real mean, and some real sharp; but I looked around in the shadows to find the quiet ones. There I let my eyes park.

Immediately I picked up my mirrors and strapped them across my face. "Looking at them is dangerous," I reminded myself. But I wanted to observe them closely. I looked at the old rain and wind-worn wall as I focused in on the shadows of their home. "How many gladiators have I fought like them?" I quietly asked myself. I counted the numbers as they clicked off in my mind. Piles of them lay broken in the shadows of my past. "Out-foxing those bastards is a difficult thing to do," I sat there and thought. I thought about the struggles and the fights. I thought of my desire for honor amid this sea of treachery. I thought of my respect for life; and, yet, my desire to live. As I looked around the shadows I identified the treacherous ones. My mind pointed out the swords of my enemies.

"Even now they track me," I thought. They continuously attempt to scale my defenses. They scheme to penetrate the ranks of my friends so they can poison the well; but my guards are strong. They campaign against me and tell people I'm too smart. They brand me as an enemy of my people. I looked around at that unrelenting war as I pretended to look into the sky. "I am a man of peace," I sat there and thought. "God, why do I have to be a warlord?"

I turned around and looked at the scruffy gladiator. "What did you say to me? How do I deal with the treacherous ones?" I looked deeply into his eyes. "I handle them very carefully," I said with a smile. We both sat there and laughed; but the laughter did little to erase the vividness of past encounters.

Most vivid was a conversation I had with a young gladiator many years prior. He was always snapping at people like a young alligator. From time to time I patted him on the head. He never forgot. And now there he stood, several years later, telling me of a scheme to murder me. He whispered in my ear, "I want to save your life."

He told me of an extremely treacherous one that loved a hesheboy. He said they planned to murder me so they could trick Caesar into setting the hesheboy free. When he told me who the gladiator was I felt my child spring alive. I felt him tremble deep inside. We knew of the gladiator's past and the depth of his treachery. The scheme that they planned was certainly an evil touch. The treacherous gladiator would wait for me in the shadows underneath the steps and he would murder me while the hesheboy watched. No one would know who did it.

While Caesar's men were confused with

pressure to solve the crime, the hesheboy would go to them to barter. In Caesar's court they call it "plea-bargaining." You do for them and they do for you. The hesheboy would testify against the treacherous one who murdered me in exchange for his freedom. "The hesheboy would then go free, to live in Rome," he said. The treacherous one would then receive a life sentence - he already had five. And then from Rome the hesheboy would send the treacherous one money for the rest of his life.

The reason they focused on me as their victim was because they knew that Caesar, and the citizenship of Rome, despised me. They rationalized that if they murdered me Caesar would not get mad and perhaps even look at my death as a blessing. Through that social sentiment the villain would jump through the loop and escape the death sentence. Their scheme against me was quite good. This would be one gladiator fight Caesar wouldn't see. It was up to me to stop it.

That night when the sentries locked me in my cell, I laid in the dark and thought of my alternatives. My child shivered and trembled; I knew the plot for my death was real, and near. "Murder him; you can get him before he gets you," pleaded my child. I tossed and turned. "But then Caesar and the citizenship would label me the treacherous one," came the answer of objectivity. "Surely they would hang me back on the cross." I looked at my child. "What about God? What would he do?" I wondered.

"You could always go to Caesar's guard

and tell them about the scheme," I thought.
"No," came the reply. "That won't work
either." They would place me in the dungeon
to protect me from harm; there I would rot
away to nothing. I would never be able
to come out again. All the gladiators would
despise me for siding with Caesar's men;
eventually they would figure out how to kill
me. I reached down for my sword and I gazed
upon its point. I thought about the threat
of death. I looked over at my hatchet. I've
carried it for twenty-five years. "Right now
the schemers are blind, they don't know you
know," came the whispers from my mind.
"You can get them before they get you,"
I thought. I laid there scheming.

"Are there any real alternatives?" I
wondered. My mind began to race. I felt
the racket rocking as my child kicked in the
gears; the wheels were spinning. I began
to think creatively. I rearranged the mental
structures and looked for new angles. I
flipped them here and there and back again.
My child went through every motion looking
for the key that would click the right
combination. We boiled down the murderous
motivation into a three-sectioned key. The
prongs were greed, fear, and jealousy. "Those
are the buttons we'll push," I told my child.
"It's only a puzzle," I tried to assure him.
But he was restless and I could feel his
muscles quiver. "We have three days before
he plans to strike," I told him in a comforting
tone. "We even know what shadow he'll
stand in." I told him to relax; that I was
in control. He shivered and shook all night

long and watched me as I slept.

Early the next day I gathered some gladiator friends. I told them I wanted a historical perspective of this treacherous one's life. They went into the arena to gather some facts and they came back with a list. Inside me my child stirred. He had never been asleep. The gladiators gave me the treacherous one's height, his weight, and the strength of his frame. They gave me the measurements of the seams in his armor and how wide they were. "Thin, disciplined, and precise thrusts," they said. I made a mental note. They told me of his weapons and the style of his attack. They told me of his gimmicks and the illusionary smile. They told me of his deceit and his disarming good nature. They told me he had murdered five good men. "He cut their throats and then spat in their blood. He walked away without giving it a thought," they told me. "Everyone he's stalked lay dead in their grave," I was reminded. The gladiators stood there looking at me. "What will you do?" they asked.

I told them to go back into the pit to collect more facts. "I want to know more about his behavior. I want to know what he eats and who he eats with. I want to know how he relaxes and who he relaxes with. What does he buy and what does he like? How does he spend his time? What are his problems and what are his fears?"

They came back again to deliver the facts and all of their faces were stern. "Buddy, let's go kill him now," they said.

I pushed that thought aside and asked them for the report. "He likes the hesheboys, and they have him deep in debt. He gambles to buy them trinkets, and they keep him emotionally upset. He buys them fine gold-laced panties of the see-through kind, and he is so deeply in love with them that they have stripped him of his mind." They went on to tell me that many gladiators were asking to be paid the money he lost to them. He was ducking and dodging, giving them a friendly grin. The social pressure on him was great and they said he planned to use me to solve his problems. I looked at them, all good men. "What will you do?" they asked.

"Gentlemen, I have a three-pronged key. I will strike him first with fear." I asked them to go back into the pit, but this time I gave them a mission. I sent them as a group to stand and talk by the treacherous one. I instructed them to let him hear what they said, but to pretend they did not know he listened. They went and talked about me and what a good man I was. They talked of how many friends I had. They talked back and forth about the strength of my wit. They said in every slave pit the gladiators liked me and if anyone ever struck me down he would have no place to hide. "He is a good, strong man," they said. The treacherous one stood there with his ear in the wind pretending he was not listening; but he never missed a sound. When they came back to me they had a big grin; they chuckled and laughed about the trap they set. "Let him think about that for a while," I told them.

All through the night my child was quiet. "We have one more day to finish our plan," I told him. I laid upon my broken bed. My child would not speak back. I tried to prod him, joke with him, love him, even start a fight; but he remained quiet as he creatively considered the alternatives.

Late in the evening on the second day I sent for the treacherous one. I laid my trap. I sent him a message by a trusted friend telling the treacherous gladiator that I uncovered a murderous plot against him. My friend told him I wanted to see him so I could help him save his life. Now I sat on that old splintered bench, covered with hard armor. Underneath my shirt was a sword-proof vest. My child made it to give me added protection. He took the sheets and tore them into strips and rolled up magazines and wove them together. Now I sat on the splintered bench, magazines rolled up tightly and woven around my chest. The only sword I had was the sharpness of my mind. I sat there calculating and watching him come near.

Toward my path he walked and I knew he contemplated my death. He stopped short of a touch and bowed his head slightly, as if to offer respect. But death was in his eyes and he could not hide from my gaze. He made an attempt to evade me by throwing his eyes on the floor, figuring that would disorient me. His disposition frightened me and I could feel my heart beat a faster rhythm. Automatically I attempted to lower the beat by breathing deeply and slowly. I consciously reminded myself that panic was ineffective. Regardless, the symptoms began to manifest. I told my child to calm down. Sweat in the palms of my hands told me the mounting stress was high, and a tendency to strike him first began to build.

I thought of the death dance between the Cobra and the Mongoose. My gaze penetrated the darkness of his eyes. I looked for the primitive spark that would signal his movement. "The reptilian brain," I thought. The tight intensity in the muscles of his jaws told me frenzy was being suppressed. But he looked at me and smiled. With my peripheral vision I gazed at the men who surrounded him; but he did not know they were there. I looked into him more deeply, aggressively running my mind through the channels of his brain. "My spirit haunts him," I thought as I watched his eyes slide under his eyebrows. His body language told me he would not strike in that moment; but I watched for the next.

Again I thought of the death dance between the Cobra and the Mongoose. I stood up from the old, splintered wooden bench and the intuition from my young child tightened the tension in my hind legs. I could feel them become free-flowing. More intuitive sophistication developed in the structure of my mid-section. Slightly it twisted so I could fling the flow of my energy like a sharp-edged rock from a sling. "Nature is my computer," I thought. "How did the Mongoose win?" I questioned the computer

board precisely. I remembered observing the
Cobra and the Mongoose fighting, but they
moved like a blur. My young child sat at
the creative engine and slowed down the
memorized movements so I could analyze.
I processed the memory of the movements
of both the Cobra and the Mongoose and
found stimulus as the key to response; the
Mongoose had conditioned him. The Mongoose
established a pattern as it swayed back and
forth. It repeated the ritualized pattern over
and over again to hypnotize the primitive
reptilian brain. The Mongoose conditioned
the Cobra to that pattern. Then, in a split
second, the Mongoose reversed his pattern
of attack. He snatched the Cobra from
the back and violently yanked him from the
ground. The Cobra hissed and spit its venom
in the air at an illusion while the Mongoose
violently snapped its back and flung it here
and there. I kept my gaze in the eyes of
this treacherous one. "Must he die?" I
wondered.

The men who surrounded him watched
his every movement. Each one was hand-
chosen and they knew death was near. I
didn't look at them but I knew they were
secretly viewing him. "How can I disengage
this process?" became a flowing torment of
my mind. "Am I handling this recklessly?"
I questioned myself. "Are there alternatives?"
I wondered. My mind continuously processed
data as I looked into his eyes.

At that moment God cast a real deep
calm inside my spirit. I knew the deck was
stacked and I saw the winning hand; my

creative machine had spit out a three-pronged key - fear, greed, and jealousy. "Strike at him and condition him," the Mongoose whispered to me. I looked deep into the Cobra's eyes and smiled as I stepped close to his right. I was told that was his strongest side and so I broke his leverage by crowding him. He tried to back up but I clipped him there with the bite of my touch. It was a soft, friendly pat on his shoulder as I spoke. "How are you doing today, brother?" He looked suspiciously into the depth of my mirrors but could find no gaze but his own. "It has been a while since I have seen you. Where have you been?" I asked as I reached down and shook his hand. His disorientation showed, and he was slightly disarmed. I watched him rare back so he could focus his gaze. Desperately he looked for the thrust of my key. But I crowded him again.

"Strike at him and shape him some more," the Mongoose said. "Give him no rest," he emphasized. Again, I looked deeply into the serpent's black and empty eyes; and I laid down a thrust with a prong of my key. "I heard you are in trouble," I said, "and that you are deep in debt." "I heard some whispers from some gladiators, and they're in love with your hesheboy. You are deep in debt to them and you can't pay back the money so they plan to take your hesheboy. On the side, when you're not around, the hesheboy lays down with them," I told him. I watched him hiss and spit his poison. It penetrated the air like a stream of fire. I looked deep into his face and saw his rage.

I danced around him and swayed back and
forth. I raised my gaze to look down on him.
"Strike at him and condition him,"
the Mongoose repeated. "I know you're
mad," I said to him, "but that's not all."
"Your hesheboy, and the gladiators, too,
have schemed a treacherous plot to murder
you. They are afraid of you and think you
should die." I stepped back and observed
him closely and watched him spit his venom.
"I don't want you to look now, but to our
left one of them stands watching you," I said
with a concerned look. He turned and looked
the other way.

My conditioning was now complete.
"Strike at him," the Mongoose said. "Grab
him and snap his back and rip him from the
ground. Fling him here and fling him there
and stomp him into the pit."

I looked at the child in me; he was
making Mongoose sounds. I watched him dance
and sway and weave and magically tear the
air. He was in a trance and it startled
me as I heard him make these sounds. He
was dressed in a robe made of Mongoose hair
and he held a magic key. He prayed to God
and danced a song about death and right and
wrong. I watched him sing and cry out his
prayer.

I looked at the back of the Cobra's head
and thought about his death. It was a strike
I could make because he was busy looking
at his own fears. I moved behind his back
and stood there with my spear. "I could
murder him now," I said to myself as I looked
deeply into my child's fear. I looked down

into my child's being and broke the spell. "We are more than this," I told him.

I said to the treacherous one, "Let's sit down." He turned to look at me. I startled him when he turned around and found me in his shadow. I reached up and pulled down my mirrored mask and let him see my blue eyes. He smiled. I talked to him about treachery and told him about good will. I talked to him about the hesheboys and the illusions of their lies. I told him about the tricks of cards and how they could wreck your life. I talked to him about desperate men and the violence they shared. I told him, too, about my game and the illusions of my lies. I told him I knew he planned to murder me and how I spared his life. I told him how I could help him by helping him pay his debts. "We can work it out," I said to him. I looked into his eyes as he looked into mine. I had split and cracked open his foundation.

He looked at me for a long time and then he hung his head. I looked at him, a beaten man. "Would he strike anyway?" I questioned myself. I observed him closely. He looked at me and spoke of sorrow and touched me on my arm. "I'll never think of killing you again," he said to me. I looked at my child and he was silent. "What do you think?" I asked my child. He never spoke a word. The treacherous gladiator raised from that old, splintered bench and he began to walk away. He stopped, looked back, and then walked back into the darkness of his world.

Two days later there was a tremor that shook the ground. They found a dead gladiator who was attacked as he slept. Caesar's sentries were on the prowl looking for the killer. Someone had taken a piece of steel and beat at the sleeping gladiator's brains. They found hair, skin, and bones splattered all over the ground.

The treacherous one struck anyway. He just restructured his vision and found a more feeble victim. My child stirred as the word came around about the hesheboy who went to Caesar's men to testify. The hesheboy told about these brutal sounds and how his curiosity had influenced him to look from behind a box. "The treacherous one was in a frenzy, a murdering frenzy," he said. "I'll help you, Caesar," he said, "if you let me out of the pit." The hesheboy testified for Caesar and then Caesar sent him to Rome to be free. That was his reward for cooperating with Caesar.

The treacherous one went to Caesar's dungeon. They gave him another life sentence. He sat there quietly for a while waiting on his check from Rome. Pacing back and forth in that dungeon, he waited and he waited. He waited on the hesheboy, the one who wore the fine, gold-laced panties of the see-through variety. Slowly, it was said, the treacherous one went insane. One day they found him sitting in the darkest corner of the dungeon. He had lip stick on, and he was asking gladiators who walked by if he could blow them. He became a hesheboy, they said.

As for Caesar, he still does what Caesar has always done. He was tricked by an illusion and still he doesn't know. it. "Give unto Caesar what is Caesar's," they say. The gladiators snicker at him behind his back; the folly of his world. They look at Caesar in his brand new suit and watch the glittering shine of his gold. To them he is nothing more than a slave master. They return to Caesar what is his.

I heard the scruffy gladiator's sound as he began to stir. He pulled me back into the immediate drudgery of this pit. He was shaking me. "Are you okay?" he asked. Silently I looked at him. The past and the present seemed to merge. He looked at me queerly. "You sure are a strange dreamer," he said. "I like to talk to you, though."

He raised from the dust and dirt and shook my hand. "Take it easy," I said. "If you think you might truly go crazy, come back and see me again." He smiled at me. I sat there watching him weave his path back into the crowd from where he came. He disappeared amid the moving anguish. I wondered about the fear he has and why he acts crazy. And I wondered, too, if it was real as I looked around Caesar's Gladiator Pit. "What do they do and what do they think as they walk around this trap?" I sat there and wondered.

"What do we fear?" I asked myself as I sat in the dust. I looked around the pit at the gladiators as they hustled here and there, going everywhere but going nowhere. I watched them play their deceitful games

and practice the swiftness of their primitive
wit. I watched them teach the treachery
to the younger ones so they could also survive
in Caesar's crime school. I watched the
gladiators with their hungry loins pressuring
the young, innocent ones to become hesheboys.
I looked around at the intense struggle.
"Where will it end?" I wondered. I thought
about the ones who died, the ones who gave
up the struggle. "What could be more awful
than death?" I wondered. "What in life
could hurt more than death?"

5

DEATH, DYING & CAPITAL PUNISHMENT

I remembered watching broken men cry. I thought of the deaths I had seen. How many men have I watched die? How many slave cells have I slaved in? I can still hear the desperate gladiator screams. How many have celled next to me? One took fire and threw it in his own bed and then laid down to sleep. What pain was greater than the pain of that fire? One gladiator climbed to a high prison perch, stuck his arms down under his belt and dove head first into the gladiator crowd. I didn't have to look to recognize that crushing-bone sound. I tried to walk away without looking, but I looked anyway. I watched his right leg twitch and fall still. I watched him drift away from our shore and into the dead sea.

How many gladiators have hung themselves because they were inadequate to compete in Caesar's Gladiator Pit? How many men have cut their wrists and swallowed poison? I watched them swallow glass, forks and spoons, too. And how many times have I looked at the slave prison cells to find their walls splattered with blood? They cut themselves with glass, toothpaste tubes, and razors. And then in panic, like a chicken with its head cut off, they run blindly into the ragged, hundred-year-old prison walls. The walls are still just as hard - like Caesar. What was that poem I wrote a hundred years ago?

I   K N E W   H E   W O U L D   D I E

I awake to hear a song -
a familiar melody
I remember the tune -
the blues of June
I imagine the picture -
the sad picture
His mournful cry -
he would die
I knew he would die . . . .

Away - only a foot
yet, infinity.
I hear his sheets -
soft strangling sheets
Their mournful cry -
he will die
I knew he would die . . . .

I hear him sing –
the familiar melody
I imagine his picture –
the lonesome picture
His mournful cry
Mother – help me
but he will die
I knew he would die . . . .

I hear the keys –
the fumbling keys
I see his picture
My mournful cry –
he will die
I knew he would die . . . .

By Buddy Martin

Yes, I remember that poem. I referred to melody and song because to experience being next to one when they decide to hang themselves is like a very sad tune. I cannot soon forget, and I guess I never will.

I sat there in the dirt and contemplated fear. I watched the gladiators. I watched Caesar's men, too. Some spoke to me as they walked by. I thought of my own fear. I remembered hanging on that isolated old cross for five years. Caesar had left me to die, and the citizenship of Rome cheered. "What was my fear?" I thought. Mostly, I remembered the pains of losing love. That was my greatest fear – to be alone. Thinking of physical death was not my greatest fear. My greatest pain was that I had never loved

like I should have.   That was my greatest
anguish suffered   on   that   isolated   cross.
I looked into   the   ripples   of   my   memory.
"Where are those scars?" I asked.   I found
another hundred-year-old poem.

MY DEAREST HONEY

My dearest honey
Fate demands -
I depart at twelve-o-one
strapped to a death machine -
I'll then be gone.
But honey listen to my words -
before I must go
To leave my lady -
It's a heartbreaking blow.

Some men die -
without meeting a master
A destiny that's cruel -
a life with no laughter
But lady -
you filled my world
with flowers and song -
Truly I'm sorry
for the things I done wrong.

Honey -
Every second of your love
was a sparkling precious -
precious stone
A diamond
a ruby -

A pearl of my own
Each one so precious
money could never buy
I was rich –
a king
Something I can't deny.

I found –
looking into your eyes
multiple rainbows full of color
Sparkling with a radiance of ecstasy –
a beauty like no other
Overflowing with tenderness –
your eyes were for me
Unlocking a magnificent world –
with the turn of your magic key.

MY   DEAREST   HONEY
2

Honey
kissing your lips
was truly the rarest touch
A symbol of love –
a softness I miss so much
Changing to passion –
with sensations filled with desire
An erupting volcano –
setting free a raging fire.

As we entwined –
a universe of our own
You gave me a kingdom –
your love was my throne

Looking at my domain -
I saw my lady
Soft and petite -
a sexy beautiful goddess -
in all sincerity sweet.

Honey -
These last few minutes
will be the hardest of my life -
cutting through my heart
like a razor-sharp knife
But like from a god -
through your love I will heal
I can stand against the world -
with your love as my shield.

So honey -
keep in mind
You're the only god I knew -
and taking your love I will never let them do
From the darkness of the unknown -
I will worship your love
and no other woman -
will I ever be thinking of.

So honey -
what I'm saying
once more before I part -
You are my god
and will forever possess my heart.

                    By Buddy Martin "72"

        I thought of that poem and looked at my
child deep in my heart.   "Who was that

girl?" I asked of my child. "Can you
remember?" I watched him closely. He
stirred while searching deeply for an answer.
He didn't speak back to me. "She was older
than you," I said as I laughed. I was trying
to prod him. "She put scars on my heart,"
he said, "but I depended on her." I looked
at him and asked, "What did you learn from
your broken heart?" He looked at me and
a smile began to show. "I learned to be
wise," he answered. I watched his eyes
and they were sad. "What do you remember?"
I asked. "She was just a breath older than
I but the complexities of her womanhood
refused to take such things lightly. To her,
such an emotional situation was a heavy
burden. However, her love for me was much
stronger than her wisdom. Together we
bonded our hearts but my heart was fearful
of her love," he answered.

In the three years we had of togetherness
she cried with loneliness. I understood not
a word of her love, and I betrayed her a
thousand times. I know sometimes we laughed,
but mostly she cried. And through the years
that followed, as I hung on that isolated cross
waiting to die, I watched her drift further
and further away. She then came to me in
a dream.

UPON A DREAM

To me she came -
upon a dream
As I lay wounded -
sighing

She embraced my heart
My love -
I have not forsaken you
I'm unable to watch -
you dying . . . .

By Buddy Martin

Yes I remember the pain as I hung on
that old lonesome cross, that death row.
I hung there for five years waiting to die.
Even when the rain splashed onto my face
it was painful. I pondered God's creation
of mighty oceans and stared into their depth.
I saw it all in a raindrop. And, too, as
time went by, that girl drifted from my mind
as did all others. I turned my eyes toward
God's creation and asked him about my death,
but all I received in return was silence and
the echoes of my own mind. As time went
by I realized that I was alone. I hung there
slowly going insane. Deeper and deeper
I went into myself, to sit alone.

I SIT ALONE

I sit alone -
upon the chair
The straps are tight -
the room is bare
My thoughts are grim -
but will not show
For only I -
could ever know.

Down came the mask –
across my face
The straps are checked –
they're all in place
My fear is near –
I grit my teeth
The seconds pass –
like lover's grief.

I feel the charge –
my body expand
I grip the chair –
with two weak hands
At last I'm free –
the straps are gone
The loneliness –
will not go on.

They spew my ashes –
upon the ground
Amongst the flowers –
home I found . . . .

By Buddy Martin "73"

How long did I sit in the dark to think?
I climbed into every shadow of myself. How
many times did I get bit? That was my
struggle: I looked for myself so I could find
me. I fought many battles inside myself.
How often did I look at death? I must have
seen it a thousand times. I thought of me,
I thought of man, I thought of the parts we
play as we act out the struggle of destiny.
How many poems did I write thinking about

my coming death?   How many did I keep
and how many did I throw away?

I   PLAY   THE   PART

The dreary cities –
filled with litter
Air's full of smog –
tastes real bitter
People turn cold –
right from the start
But in that world –
I play no part . . . .

The rain rages –
lightening strikes
Cold winter wind –
stings and bites
Floods are cruel –
They have no heart
but in that world –
I play no part . . . .

The death chair waits –
smooth with gloss
Fate is final –
I am lost
Time is near –
for me to start
But in that world –
I play the part . . . .

By Buddy Martin

"How many times did I think of killing myself?" I wondered. Waiting to die was like standing on the chopping block waiting for the final blow from Caesar's axe. One constantly tried to imagine what death would be like, or what it would mean. How many times did I ask myself, "What will death be like?" How many times did I approach the edge of my death, look over the brink into the darkness of the unknown, and then feel God push me away from that ledge? How many times did I struggle against God to look into that dead sea? My child, in his burning curiosity, needed to know what was there. Even God couldn't keep him away until he found out. Finally, God uncloaked that darkness and showed him the unfolding secrets of eternity.

While you wait to die no one can comfort you because they can't understand. You are unable to communicate because if you touch that subject people say, "Stop it, that depresses me." They just look at you strangely and whisper to each other as they walk by. From time to time some of the bolder ones will ask for your autograph, and if they are without that courage they will send their children. How many times did I blush and say no? Or how many times, if they were persistent, did I hurriedly scribble my name across their paper so I could escape from them?

In parts of Caesar's rule they still strap you to that electrical death machine. It fries, scrambles, and sizzles your brain. The violently surging charge of electricity

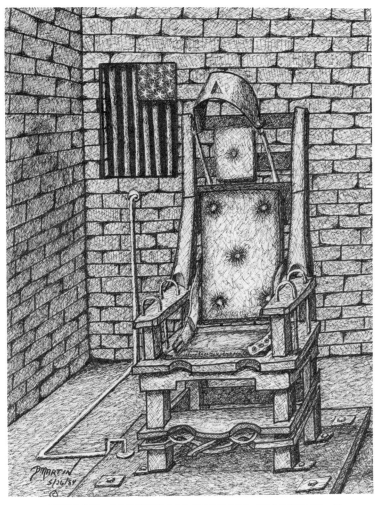

GREAT AMERICAN DREAM MACHINE II

By

Buddy Martin

tears its way through your molecules. It has such force that it makes your eyeballs pop from their sockets like corks shooting from a toy gun. Your flesh swells up and stretches until it rips open with crevices, and from there the blood boils from your life. They put a mask over your face so your tongue can't be seen stretching and slashing about with such tremendous force it rips the teeth from their roots. But now, I've heard, Caesar is growing kind. His wizards have created a new death technology.

Now they just strap you to a bed in front of a window with beautiful curtains. They slide a needle into your arm that is so sharp it can't be felt as it slides between the living molecules. Attached to the needle is a thin rubber tube hooked to a bottle of poison. You lay there waiting, and then like drama upon the stage Caesar pulls the curtain. The citizens of Rome sit there looking through the window, looking at the unfolding of Caesar's drama. The citizens suck in their breath. "Goddamn, what a thrill," they sigh. They sit on the edge of their seats and, letting the anticipated next moment run through them like unbridled anxiety in a horror movie, they go "ahhhhhhh." They sit there waiting. Anticipating.

Then comes the ring master. "Ladies and gentlemen! Due to Caesar's benevolence, the convict shall be allowed to speak his last words." The citizenship of Rome sit there, waiting. The convict now takes center stage. He can beg for forgiveness, beg for his life, cry, be tough and defiant, forgive them of their sins, or, if he wishes, be philosophical. Caesar doesn't care; it's all part of the drama. He likes variety. Down through the tube, gently creeping into the blood, comes the wizard's dark and deadly poison. The gladiator lays there, droopy-eyed, and from time to time comes a twitching muscular spasm. "See," says Caesar, "we are a gentle and humane civilization."

The press then interviews the eyewitnesses. "What was it like?" they ask. "What did you see? What did you feel?" As the citizens walk away they say, "It's been a hard day." The reporters then go out and shout the news from Caesar's highest mountains as they attempt to stir up debate and controversy. But Caesar murders so many the display is no longer shocking or controversial. Murder is not inhumane, not if Caesar does it. When Caesar does it, it is entertaining.

As for the gladiators all lined up in the shadows under the arena waiting their turn to die, they know they may get away today, if lucky, but tomorrow will come. They cling to their shields and wait. They try to imagine what it will be like to lay down and die in front of Caesar's crowd. Perhaps the last feeble echo that will register in their dying brain will be the sound of the cheer. That will be their last vision of humanity - the law that says no says yes.

For the gladiators all lined up and waiting in Caesar's shadow, death row is long. But Caesar is kind. He is always trying to devise

CAESAR'S MANIA

By Bob Cunningham

new and humane ways in which to slaughter
in a socially acceptable way. I heard he is
now busy building dog runs that are long wire
cages. He has set the cages in the sunshine
so the men can experience its warmth.
He wants them to have fresh air while they
wait to die. They can exercise by running
back and forth. The open-air cages keep
them healthy and, in their desperation, stop
them from killing one another. Caesar wants
them strong. The citizens of Rome tend to
protest when a feeble gladiator is executed.
Caesar likes to exaggerate gladiator strength.
But in reality, behind the mask of that
gladiator strength is a weak and feeble lamb
that cries for its mother. Caesar never sees
the tears they hide in the shadow. Inside
of that apparent strength is a bleeding heart
that cannot communicate. All channels of
communication have been jammed. The
gladiator is lost amid the rocky peaks of
Caesar's mountain and he doesn't know how
to come down. At the very best, he can
pretend to be strong while the wolf snaps
at his flank. Caesar doesn't realize gladiators
too are God's children.

　　　　Caesar is moralistic. Caesar gives good
examples to all of humanity about humanity.
He says, "Thou shall not kill," and then he
slaughters. He is the father smoking a
cigarette while his child watches. The child
reaches for the ashtray to be like dad and
then Caesar swats him. "That's no good for
you," he says. Caesar can't understand why
his children are confused.

　　　　I sat in the dirt, in the middle of

everyone's path, thinking. I turned my gaze
to look at Caesar's darkest dungeon. Silently,
I sat there looking. I looked at the old
bricks and thought of the men sitting in
those shadows of despair as they waited
to die. I boosted the strength of my
perceptors and let my vision penetrate
through the old brick walls, past the bars,
and into the small slave cells. As I observed
the men condemned to die, I felt their
gladiator anguish bolt through me like a
highly charged electrical current.

Systematically, I gazed from cell to cell.
I looked closely at the pencil-drawn graffito
that was grotesquely expressed like hysterical
babblings upon their dungeon walls. Some
of it was about slogans of courage in the
face of death. Some of it was defiant, angry,
depressed or wild. Sometimes Caesar's men
would paint over it in an attempt to cover
up the documented anguish and madness.
However, it would quickly be replaced with
a new expressive tide of human struggle.
Some of it had been scraped into the surface
plaster, forming deeply grooved and well
traveled roads of neurotic activity. Their
art was desperate. The agony of their
expressions was frightening and reminded me
of primal and primitive scenes. "Cave
paintings," I thought to myself.

I let my eyes scan the rows of
condemned men. Some were writing, reading,
shaving; and some were silently crying. Others
were hollering from cell to cell. They talked
about their past, or the things they knew.
What they all shared was living with the

agony of a condemned mind. They tried to
relax but the thought of death engulfed them
and surrounded them like fish trapped in a
knotted net. These men who are on a schedule
with death constantly grapple in desperation
to maintain their sanity.

I watched them slowly dying. I knew
the mental anguish well. Their fantasies are
about freedom and the lives they could have
had. They see themselves with their women,
their children, and the lifestyles they desire.
Then the thought of death intrudes into their
consciousness. Fact and fantasy, meaning
and meaninglessness, echo back and forth in
their minds. They work themselves into
a frenzy as they attempt to solve equations
that have no solution. They begin to
hyperventilate, sweat gathers in the palms
of their hands, and their heartbeat quivers
with fibrillation. "I'm dying!" comes the
scream from within themselves.

They feel the net being drawn tighter
as some develop symptons of hypochondria.
Cancer begins to form in their jaws, and in
their spines. They cough, quiver, and the
tension in their backs tightens with sharp
sensations of pain. Crystals of broken and
jagged glass become scattered throughout their
brains.

Caesar sends his wizard of psychiatry
to see what is wrong. The psychiatrist
projects his human concern. He talks softly,
soothing, and asks if he can be of assistance.
"It's all a problem of attitude," he concludes.
Then he gives them a magic potion that
makes them snicker and laugh as they lay

down to dream.

Each of those who is condemned to die is locked tight in the dark, dreary dungeon. They have to die. They have no alternative. From time to time their thoughts drive them insane. They either fall into pure rage, deep depression, or a state of confusion that renders them highly assaultive and unpredictable. Some of them descend into deep states of psychosis. They vanish amid the mental abstractions of an incomprehensible living universe of suffering.

But Caesar is kind. He responds by putting magic light boxes called televisions in the condemned men's dungeon cells. It is said these will prevent the majority of the imprisoned gladiators from going insane. Since the men are so deeply deprived and restricted from contact with the outside world, Caesar replaces real human contact with the illusions of make-believe.

All the gladiators have to do is push a button and organized structures of light radiate out of that magic light box. The box spins out fast moving pictures that projects illusionary representations of a world known as modern day society. It is really a magical event when that box clicks on. It shows an advanced civilization where people dress real strangely and the city streets are alive with human adventure that is purposeful and meaningful. The human spirit looks as though it is alive and well. All one has to do is plug in mentally and pretend that they are among the characters on the screen. The people are dancing, girls are looking good.

There are children; small, loving and innocent looking children who hug and kiss their happy parents. That magic light box is the strangest thing I have ever seen. It provides illusionary and tranquilizing dreams. It prevents the condemned gladiators from killing themselves before Caesar does. Caesar is smart. He knows how to preserve.

I backed my gaze out of those dark and agonizing human shadows. I looked into myself. Yes, when they removed me from Caesar's death list, when they cut me down from that intense human terror, I guess God had another destiny planned for me. I reflected into my past. I saw the long, jagged, and twisted road of human suffering that my child and I had traveled. I looked at my child and observed him closely looking back at me. I thought of our struggles, our adventures and our companionship. "God, I would have never made it without his creativity being near," I thought.

I sat there and thought of the time he stole Caesar's books. He must have stolen five hundred of them and hid them in my prison cell. He had all of the bureaucrats in Caesar's land looking for them. Somehow he figured out how to sneak past the sentries who guarded Caesar's book store. He gained access to the computer and pushed all kinds of buttons that sent books to my door. He told me to read them to him so he could understand. He laid there listening for days, months, and years. He began to show me new creative things.

I looked at him and said, "You got

pretty smart, didn't you fella? Who would
ever believe you came from Caesar's darkest
slums?" I began to prod him. "What do
these gladiators fear?" I asked. He pulled
some books from his mind, some of the ones
he stole from Caesar. He systematically
flashed through the indices; he knew every
angle. "This world is dark and dim in here,"
my child responded. "It is difficult to see.
Our nature has been stripped bare and here
we're forced to fight. Caesar knows about
this world. I read it in his books. He knows
that men in desperate states are subject to
aggressiveness. We are social animals and
through our nature we have human needs.
We are the mirror of man, and we reflect
those needs. Living in Caesar's Gladiator
Pit strips us of the essential elements needed
to create a positive and productive direction.
What the world wants us to be is that which
is denied. We are unable to see, feel, or
understand. We are unable to reflect what
we do not have. What surrounds us is what
we become."

6

RON & LEROY

We live in Caesar's Gladiator Pit and here we struggle to survive. We mold our armor and fight our fights amid a violent sea of confusion. If we wish to live we must scheme. When man is stripped of his love for life he must fight. And Caesar strips them all - naked.

Most of the men start out clinging to their dreams. But slowly as time goes by cruelty dims their sensibilities. They try like hell to love; but slowly, as time goes by, that love becomes a weakness. It is difficult to be tender and swing a sword at the same time. Gladiators learn that to survive in the pit you must fight the impulse to love.

What do we fear? We fear many things. We fear we will lose our minds amid this sea of distortion. Some struggle to cling to the higher forms of human concern but surviving in this reality forces one to let

them go.   Slowly, what sensitivity we had
is stripped away.   That world out there and
this in here are not the same.   The rules
are different; and if we don't harden, we
die.

Slowly our world becomes darker.   Our
bonds are ripped and torn apart as we become
gladiators.   We pull back into ourselves.
And from that foundation comes alienation.
In that loneliness we lose the love for life.
Then our own nature turns against us; to be
alone is not natural.   With this posture we
survive, but because of natural human law
we die.   Man was not meant to walk alone.
In loneliness man decays.   Slowly, darkness
turns to pain.   The forces of isolation shatter
us like broken glass.   With the fragments
we kill ourselves to give us peace at last.
This is the gladiator's fate.   This is what
gladiators fear most.

I raised myself up from the dirt and
stretched my muscles toward God's sky.
I raised all the way up to the tips of my
toes and stretched every muscle until they
popped into place.   I squeezed my energy
forcefully and screamed, "I'm alive!"   I let
my words echo and bounce around on Caesar's
old brick walls.   I turned around and looked
at the gladiators as they stared at me like
I was insane.   "God, I don't know about all
of this," I said to myself.   "What gives me
my hope and courage?"   I looked at my
child intently.   "Our dreams have not died,"
I said.   He looked at me and laughed.   "Go
get Caesar's key," he said, "I must be set
free."

"Oh yes, young boy," I thought, "you
are a dreamer." "The dreams you have are
golden ones. Even as you walk amid the
shadows of Caesar's gallows, you have the
courage to dream. You still cling to that
love for life and you love to create, too.
Caesar frightens you but still you go forward
to dream. Did you ever notice when Caesar
comes around he fears to look at you? Why
do you think that is?" My child reached over
and touched Caesar's books. "Caesar knows
I know," he said. "Caesar won't look at me
because he fears to look at himself."

I looked around for Ron over on punk-
iron row. He was not to be found. I turned
and walked toward the corner of an old cell
block. From there I could view other sections
of the gladiator pit. I stopped in the shadows
so I could better see into the bright light.
I observed Ron hunched down, surrounded by
slaves, and in the center of a gladiator marble
game.

Without wondering, I knew he was
winning. I walked toward the game but
didn't stop. The child in me kicked Ron's
sword as I walked by. I walked to a
perspective where I could observe the marble
game without letting them know I was
watching. I looked around at the sentries
and leaned up against an old wooden box.
Ron knew I was there but no one else did.

I watched them play their marbles.
Caesar didn't allow the gladiators to have
money so they devised their own economic
system. With those marbles one could buy
anything within the dimensions of Caesar's

Gladiator Pit. For six marbles you could
fuck a hesheboy. You could buy swords
and armor. You could buy food, magic smoke,
wine, or extra blankets for your bed.
Anything to be found within the circle of
this pit could be bought with those marbles.
Those marbles were the currency of the
gladiator economy.

I watched Ron's skill. He stirred up
the gladiator's emotions so he could distract
them. They argued with one another over
the thrust of his remarks, and then under
the shadow of his skillful hands the marbles
disappeared one by one. No one saw his
theft but me. They all watched the marbles
closely, like hungry hawks, but Ron made
the snatch right in the center when the light
was in their eyes.

I stood there unobtrusively as a non-
participant observer watching the movement
of Ron's magic. When he couldn't create
a blind spot to steal from, he relied on his
skill. He calculated the angles. And then
with graceful form he shot his shooter to
knock his target from the circle. He then
placed the marble into his already stuffed
pockets. I watched his shrewdness and his
struggle to survive.

Ron was an orphan boy. He came
from Caesar's slums. As he grew up he
drifted from house to house looking for his
roots. He had a thousand homes, but yet
he had none. He struggled among the alleys
and slept in the all-night movie houses. He
snatched food from here and there and ran
from the spears of Caesar's men. Once he

almost died when he had nothing to eat.

I remembered the day they brought him in - a hundred years ago. He was so thin I couldn't take my eyes off of him. He was a white-yellow pale and his skin laid upon the surface of his bones. Never before had I seen a man so lean. I had been hungry before but never like him. I watched him everywhere he went. He was white, but when he talked he sounded black. "I was raised in Caesar's black ghettos," he said. "I was tried in Caesar's court as a black man. But in reality I'm just a dirty white boy."

I viewed him for months, secretly watching him. One night I needed some marbles and got into a game. As the game progressed, I noticed the marbles I tried to steal disappeared before I could get them. I looked around and began to focus suspiciously on the shadows in the game. I watched Ron and I observed his tricky fingers pretend they were doing one thing while in reality they were doing another. I didn't say a word. My child was delighted. He wanted to play.

I decided to take a gamble so I quickly darted my hand into the shadows (in a way that couldn't be seen by normal perception) to steal a marble. My child waited. Without notice, he watched Ron closely. The child could tell by the way the tension in Ron froze that he was caught. But Ron never spoke a word. That moment fused our bond. He and I shared a different world; we were gifted.

I was heavily into drugs then. I swallowed anything to escape Caesar's pain.

I swallowed, snorted, and injected. I was
lost in a sea of emotional and psychological
devastation. I tried every way I could to
escape the pain of Caesar's world. I walked
around in the shadows numb and dumb.
I laid down in my slave cell and pumped
morphine deep into the chambers of my mind.
It flooded into my life like a magic potion
as I laid down to dream.

   Under the spell of morphine I learned
to control my mind. I lay motionless on
my broken bed and let sweet visions drift
slowly through my brain. When that bored
me, I asked my mind if it could run things
backwards. Without hesitation visions appeared
in reverse. I was amazed. I gave my mind
greater challenges. Could it shuffle things
around and give me fragmented sequences?
Fragmented visions poured forth. My brain
did anything I asked. That was when I first
rediscovered my child. After many years
of hiding, he came back to me. Where is
that poem I wrote a hundred years ago?

FELL   OF   AMBROSIA

   While standing on the moor –
   by the fell of ambrosia
   With soul way-worn,
   the paradox of being
   Mind enchained –
   from all I was seeing
   I pulled out a spike –
   decided to rest

Morphine it was –
could it pass the test?
Make the fell of ambrosia –
seem only a jest?
While standing on the moor –
by the fell of ambrosia . . . .

By Buddy Martin

That was how I spent all my marbles.
I stayed stoned.   There was no pain, just a
flowing magical world where there were
quiet dreams.   The world around me was
ripping and tearing apart, but in its center
I found peace.   Oh, what a sweet sweetness.
    Once, I pulled Ron to the side.   He
was blowing notes from his magic flute.
I talked him into mixing the morphine with
his blood.   He looked at me suspiciously, but
he did.   I watched him return to his flute
but the sounds were no longer there.   He
became agitated and ran to his slave cell
to lock himself in.   He complained for days
about that crazy stuff.   "It made me sick,"
he said.
    One day I ran upon some hippy
gladiators and they gave me some small,
square pieces of paper.   They said magic was
on them and I took them to Ron to share.
We ate them.   I watched Ron begin to act
strangely; he ran in circles.   He then
repeatedly ran up and down some steps.   He
was confused and he didn't know where to
go.   He became absent-minded.   He went

in one direction and then in another. Finally, he ran to his slave cell and locked himself in. I stood there giggling and howling with laughter. Never in my life had I seen anything so funny.

But then a strange thing happened – monsters poured from my brain. My mind worked so fast I couldn't keep up with it. It flashed thousands of images and pictures, all within seconds. The flood of information overran my consciousness and my control rapidly broke down. I scrambled toward my cell with monsters hot in pursuit. I locked myself in but the monsters followed. In that small cell I battled them all night long. That was the first time I ever sincerely prayed. "Please, God, make it stop and I promise I'll never take it again," I pleaded. "Damn hippies, what kind of crazy shit was that?" I wanted to hit them with my sword for many years thereafter.

As the years went by Ron and I bonded together to hustle the marble games. We hustled every gladiator there was, including the most treacherous ones. We picked their pockets and stripped them clean. We left them broke, bare, and deeply in debt. But that game grew so old to me. I watched the gladiators in their stupidity; they believed our illusions. As fast as they laid down their marbles, I snatched them from their vision and stuffed them in my pockets. I covered Ron's shadow while he made his illusive moves, and then he covered mine.

I watched the gladiators and their anguish as I robbed them. I looked deep into their eyes and could feel their cries. "They are all trying to rob me," I thought. "Why should I care?" But there was such deep pain and sorrow, and as time went by I could no longer bear that pain. I backed away from the marble game. I backed away from the hard drugs, too. My child brought me Caesar's books. I went to my cell and stayed for years. I gave Ron some of Caesar's books, too.

One day I said to Ron, as a joke, "Let's go take a high school test." Ron got blasted on some magic smoke, and, giggling, we went to the gladiator schoolhouse. It was only a joke, but we passed. We were now high school graduates and we had diplomas to prove it. "What do you think about college?" I asked him. He looked puzzled. I was almost thirty years old and he was already past that. I went on to college and a few months later he slid into the desk behind me. "It's a good hustle," he said. "I can collect G.I. benefits." We went on to school and unexpectedly our education turned quite serious. We met some people who were extremely sensitive and they really cared. Skillfully they guided our minds along. They turned us into philosophizing gladiators. I graduated from Penn State University with a degree in sociology. Ron needs another course and he too will graduate.

From my thoughts I drifted back into focus on the marble game. I looked at Ron and made a mental note to aggravate him about that last college course, the unfinished goal. To my right I caught fast gladiator movement. I watched the gladiators as they ran from the shadow against the wall and ran behind a slave cell block. I couldn't see what was going on. I walked to where I could get a better view. Two gladiators were beating each other with baseball bats and they were both covered with blood. All the other gladiators formed a circle around them and cheered them on.

"Take the pussy," they shouted. That was their way of expressing masculine domination. Whoever won symbolically fucked the other. The loser took on the feminine role. To be beaten was to lay with your legs open and be dominated by the powerful erection of the victorious one. I quietly watched the bloodbath. The dark screaming sounds of howls from the gladiators echoed our primal ancestry. Their pitch was sharp and wild. It triggered in me a primitive feeling. I felt a roar from deep inside of me. Quickly I looked down into my child. He was now a wild, roaring lion and he raged with violent aggression. He slammed against the cage. Viciously he clawed at the bars and tore at the floor. In haste I walked back to where I had watched Ron in the marble game.

I kept trying to calm my child down; but he was emotionally out of control. "Hey, hey, hey," I yelled, trying to get him to focus on me. He was trapped in the emotional rhythm of the primal past and I had to pull him closer to me. "Everything is okay," I said. "You are not at war." I kept gently poking at him with my logical prod. "Think of Beverly," I said. "Think of me, think of us." Slowly, he came out of his hypnotic trance. It was as if he were dazed and looked into a primitive past where his perceptions became so strong he became what he saw. "Everything is okay," I said. "You are safe. I guard you. I protect you. Look at me. We are okay." I watched him quiver and slowly calm down. I watched his fangs turn back into teeth and his claws turn back into fingernails. "We are okay," I repeated.

I looked just to my right and saw Leroy standing in a group of black warrior gladiators. He stood at attention. All of his senses were alert. I stood in my spot, quietly and unobtrusively, analyzing the warriors who surrounded him. As a black nation they were soldiers and they fought a holy war.

They were a tight-knit group and they had their own guards posted to the left and right of them. They stood against the hundred-year-old brick wall. I watched Leroy standing there, real neat and clean. "Discipline," I thought. The thoughts of Leroy stirred my child. "I want to go play with that little nigger-boy," he said. Before I realized it, my steps were taking me toward the tribe of black warriors.

As I approached, Leroy noticed me and broke from their ranks. He walked toward me with a happy smile on his face. We met against the wall. "Brother Leroy," I heard my child say, "I'm thinking of working on a project." "It will be a short story with illustrations about Caesar's Gladiator Pit. I was thinking about describing you as a small Pygmy man who Caesar captured among the vines of Africa's jungle. What do you think about that?"

My child chuckled deeply inside myself. He watched brother Leroy's facial expressions intently. Leroy glanced around to see if anyone had heard. And as if other gladiators were standing too close, he pulled my arm and said, "Come on over here, Buddy, I want to talk with you." Inside myself my child was howling with laughter but he kept a straight and serious face.

"What if they turn it into a drama or a play upon the stage?" he asked. "Everyone will laugh and ridicule me." My child looked at Leroy and laughed. "Maybe they will turn it into a ballet with a black Pygmy swooping across the stage. How would you like that?" my child asked. Leroy nervously glanced around and then he, too, started to laugh. He made a few body gestures and then shuffled his feet like he was a midget with a three-prong pitchfork stabbing at his feet. We both laughed, and laughed some more.

I looked seriously at him so I could capture his character in my mind. He was approximately five-foot-two in height. He was a real proud and perceptive black man. He was captured in the black slums of Caesar's ghetto and he carried a strong torch of burning curiosity. He was gifted. But with his physical height and build he was small and fragile looking. However, when he spoke, all his black brothers came to attention. Underneath his child-like appearance he was a commander. He had the eyes of a hawk and the perceptive nervous system of a finely tuned biological machine.

He constantly asked a million questions; then he took the answers back to his black warrior brothers. "We need your knowledge," he told me, "so we can survive." I found him to be an extremely sensitive human being, and my child loved him.

I observed him closely on a logical and analytical plane while my child constantly prodded him with all kinds of creative gestures and illusive tricks. My child was forever testing his perceptions. Ron and I poured information into him like he was a dry sponge. He absorbed it all. I looked at him sincerely. "I would never betray your character," I promised.

He was one of the guards God gave me, and when he guarded me he was a highly disciplined soldier. Not that I ever asked him to be my guard; God just put him there from time to time. Whenever I stepped from my slave prison cell, or stepped into the gladiator pit, he would be near. And he would look so serious as he stood on guard. There was no shadow that could escape the penetration of his gaze.

"Come and talk to my brothers," he said. "Show them your visions and let them see your world." Relentlessly, he pulled at me and dragged me into his black tribe. My child was nervous among that camp. He always looked into their faces looking for the nigger-boy who shot him with a blank gun when he was a baby. "Talk to my brothers," brother Leroy said.

I stood there against the wall looking at him, thinking about his magic. "He could be a great black leader someday," I thought. All he needs is the proper kind of education. I talked to him about the world and I poured as much information into him as I could. I talked to him about goals, organization, structure, motivations, perceptions, sensitivity, courage, and greatness. I talked to him about creativity and finding solutions to novel, complex problems. "Brother Leroy," I said, "I'm on a mission and I must go." "I'll see you tomorrow and we'll talk again." I patted him on the back as he turned to walk back to his tribe.

I spun around and walked back to the old wooden box where I could once again view the marble game. I stood there on guard. "Ron is a hustler," I thought. "He has it in his blood." He still hustles those marble games, relentlessly. When I quit playing our partnership remained. He loved a real good game. Half those marbles coming out of that pot were mine. And Ron invented a million games with a million pots. "He is highly conscious of currency," I thought. "We cannot survive and live without it," he would say. Of course he's right; but I lost my spirit for the game.

I liked to play with art but you couldn't make any money at it. And besides, usually when I finished a piece of art, I fell so deeply in love with the spirit of it that I didn't want to sell it. I liked to make paintings and sculptures. They gave me real good dreams. Ron hustled the

marbles while I played with my paints. And
when he found time, he painted too. We
did our art and dreamed about a greater
world; a world of beauty. We constantly
exchanged ideas. I stood there watching him
in that marble game.

We were friends for so many years; we
went way back. We clashed on many
occasions, him believing one thing and me
believing another. We pulled out our swords
in heated debate and slammed them violently
against one another creating such intense
sparks they could have set the world on fire.
Once we went for a year without speaking.
But through all that time, as we watched
one another in silence, we quietly guarded
each other.

Neither one of us allowed the other
to make a mistake. If one did the other
would pounce on it to rip it apart and then
scatter it to the wind. That is how we
taught each other. We allowed no distortions,
no inaccurate information, no illusions, no
lies, no deceptions; we commanded and
demanded nothing but accuracy. We knew
to accept anything less opened the door to
vulnerability. Yes, we had high standards;
but that was the discipline of our friendship.
That was our bond, our trust, and our faith.

He worked with me through the weekday
in Caesar's ceramic shop. We were slaves
there, working for pennies a day. Caesar
manipulated our talents and sold our work
to the citizenship of Rome. We were artists;
that was our profession. We met first thing
in the morning. We quietly compared notes

about Caesar's environment; what took place recently and any major changes or projections for the future were discussed. We worked together like a unified calculator with two brains. Nothing took place in Caesar's Gladiator Pit without us knowing about it. And from that position we fashioned our dreams.

Together we studied, built, and grew. We each had our own goals and viewpoints but together we struggled against the forces that surrounded us. We struggled within the dimensions of our own living circumstances. We struggled to solve the complexity of our personal problems. We knew this reality, we knew it well; that was why we bonded together and synchronized our thoughts. We knew that cooperation built a stronger defense. Together we enhanced our probability of survival.

I stood there in the dust and dirt and watched Ron in that marble game. My child regarded him his closest companion. My child always looked at him kindly. I watched Ron shoot his marbles and stuff his pockets. I was not really concerned that anything would go wrong as I stood on guard. He was highly skilled at social manipulation. He knew how to communicate extremely well and he knew how to fashion the gladiator minds. He took them all for a wild and gleeful ride, stuffed his pockets, and left them loving him.

"And how many times have I watched him help the other gladiators?" I wondered. Whenever they came to him broke and in debt, he freely gave. He lectured them and taught them about life. He talked about values, a strong sense of morality, and the right path for humanity. He told them about learning, planning, and growing; and he carried their burdens when they were too heavy for them. From time to time his temper flared and he became aggressive but it never lasted long. He carried no grudge. I stood there watching him, closely, shooting his marbles. "What will his future be, God?" I asked. "Will Caesar kill him?"

I turned to my right and walked to the old rain and wind-worn wall. From there I could see better. I saw just about all of Caesar's Gladiator Pit; and, too, could still watch the marble game. I leaned against the wall. "God, I am so weary," I thought. My shield was heavy. I watched Ron glance around to find my new location. He raised up from the marble game stuffing his already full pockets and he walked toward me grinning. I heard the loud steel bell ring. It signaled the end of the exercise period. I breathed a sigh of relief.

I watched the gladiators step from the shadow of that one hundred year old wall and file toward the big, wide gate. Ron walked up to me and handed me two handfuls of marbles. We both laughed and snickered. We stood by the wall stalling, waiting for the gladiator pit to thin out. Then as the last two gladiators, we fell in at the rear and marched back through that big wide magic steel door. Toward the future it hurled us; back into contemporary time.

CAESAR'S STRONGHOLD
By
Ron Connolly

7

HUMAN
DEVASTATION

    Into the loudly echoing prison corridors
I walked. The stench of crowded and cagey
living conditions infiltrated the nostrils of
my mind. "Surrounded," I thought, as I
looked at the guards stationed on my left
and on my right. Ron and I walked through
the shadows toward our prison cells. I
watched the bright sunlight bounce off the
dark shadows it couldn't penetrate. When
we reached a separation in the catacombs
Ron turned left and I turned right. "Catch
ya tomorrow in the slave yard," I said.
"Do you need anything?" he asked. "No,"
I replied. And we drifted apart.
    When I reached another branch in the
catacombs I made another right-hand turn.
As I stepped through the door into the cell
block I glanced to my left and looked at the
two telephones hanging on the hundred-year-old

walls. I thought of Beverly.   Those phones
were an important channel of communication
that linked me to the free world.   Without
them I was blocked completely from society.
It was through those phones that I struggled
to touch humanity.

I thought of the guards and how they
controlled the phones.   Some of them were
liberal and gave the inmates easy access to
the telephones.   They showed concern and
appreciation for the attempt to maintain
family and community bonds.   But others used
the phones as a means of institutional control;
another club with which to beat us.

Through those phones I became highly
sensitive to sound.   Just like a blind man who
is denied the light of day, I too developed
my sense of hearing.   By deciphering sound,
tone, and pitch, I sensed joy, pain, suffering,
insecurity, and happiness.   I recognized
deception, as well as sincerity.   I weighed
the molecules of depression through the sound
of its heavy gravity.   As soon as someone
answered the phone their mood was apparent.
Through conversation I saw the outside world.

With a heightened state of awareness
I automatically looked to my right.   I observed
a man moving up quickly behind another
who was bent over the water fountain drinking.
I immediately sensed danger.   All of a sudden
a highly perceptive and sensitive camera
turned on in my mind.   My child became a
cameraman.

He clicked away at the unfolding
sequence of events.   I watched a sharp blade
stab its way through space.   A violent man

swiftly moved up behind his target. With great force he drove the dull-gray blade into the right side of his victim's chest. The powerful thrust spread the rib cage and plowed its way toward the unsuspecting beating heart. When the hilt of the blade slammed against the chest, there was a loud, dull thud. It sounded like a man had been punched in the chest real hard. He pulled it out just as quickly as he had driven it in. The man drinking the water quickly raised and spun around to face his attacker. He thought he had been punched in the chest. Not realizing he had been stabbed, he charged his assailant as he threw up his fists.

Blood squirted from his chest like water from a ruptured pipe. It squirted and splashed everywhere. I looked deeply into his eyes as he finally comprehended his imminent death. My child clicked the pictures as the shock spread across his face. I watched the man collapse onto the butt-covered cold cement floor. He laid there having convulsions and then slid into the dark sea of death. I watched as God pulled him away from shore.

I shifted my focus, just slightly, and looked straight into the eyes of the angry attacker. His eyes were glazed with frenzy and he was frozen in both time and space. He was on the verge of going into shock himself. It was as if he were stoned on the very action of his own deed.

Slowly he turned and looked into my eyes. In that moment I knew he weighed the possibility of also killing me. I was a witness. But, too, he glanced around farther from me and saw other men watching. He realized he couldn't kill us all. Slowly he backed up and looked for an avenue of escape. He threw his weapon behind an old steam-pipe radiator and ran down the cell block. I watched him for a few seconds. In his confusion there was nowhere to run. I then turned to my left and walked briskly back to my cell.

I stepped into my prison cell, 453, and pulled the one hundred year old door shut behind me. I glanced up at Beverly's picture hanging on the wall. I laid down my sword and let down my shield. Slowly I unsnapped my armor. I glanced down at Ted's envelope as it laid upon that old wooden desk. I stood there for a few minutes listening to the wild screaming noise of the protesting inmates. I reached over and clicked on the stereo and then soaked two balls of cotton to stuff deeply into my ears. It helped me block out the insanity; it cut away the sharp edge.

I reached down and unbuckled my pants and then peeled off my shirt. I stripped off my underwear and felt the cool air from the catacombs gently brush against my nakedness. It felt so cool and so life giving. I reached down and felt around my stomach, looking for signs of flab, and then I stretched all my muscles to feel the strength of my life. "I'll be thirty-six in eight days," I told myself, "not bad." I reached around and hung a heavy coat over the cell door so I could gain some privacy, and then I laid naked upon the broken bed. Now came a challenge. I had to somehow relax and forget the day's events. Showers were in an hour.

I laid there naked. Nakedness, invariably, triggered thoughts of sexuality in me. "My nature is so damn strong," I thought. I contemplated masturbation. "I could always squirt my power onto the state-issued towel," I thought. "It would help me release my stress." The child in me had the capacity to create a million sexual fantasies. He projected them onto the screen in my brain, interwove my emotions with them, and made them unfold with an abundance of variation. "He is real creative when it comes to sex," I thought.

But logically the fantasies made me wonder, "If I pretend to make love to a woman and that woman loves me in return, who is really the woman?" "It's a strange thing the way prison societies force you to make love to yourself." Somehow, in the logic of that, I sensed that the prison administrators created a sexual degeneracy in the men they kept. By denying access to the opposite sex, they create a distortion that leads to all kinds of sexual abnormalities. I believe it leads to confusion in one's sexual identification. When the men get out on parole they do what they were taught, and then, when caught, they come back for breaking society's rules. I laid there and thought of squirting my power on Pennsylvania's state-issued towel and then flinging it into a dark corner. But I changed my mind. I remembered in the past watching

a hungry mouse climb up on that towel and
eat my unborn child.

I thought of the women Caesar sent
into this prison. Some of them he put in
the prison hospital to work as nurses, others
he made teachers. A few he even allowed
to be guards. A new law says that Caesar
cannot discriminate against hiring women.

I laid there and thought of the women
walking around the yard and through the cell
blocks. I reflected on the sight of their
feminine asses bulging against their uniforms.
There was a time when my mind associated
a guard's uniform with fear and intimidation.
Now when women guards walk by I get an
erection and sexual fantasies boil through
my brain. The feminine stimulus is certainly
a source of confusion.

A gladiator friend recently got confused.
He misinterpreted a woman guard's interaction
as caring and concern. He came to believe
that one of them wanted to make love to
him. He told her he knew she was watching
him, and wanting him. When Caesar learned
of this he was enraged. Caesar's guards
grabbed him, locked him away, and put a
strange note in his file. They said he was
suffering from "delusional jealousy." They
said he needed to be placed in administrative
custody until he could be evaluated by
Caesar's psychiatrists. They made him dress
in blue so he stood out from all the others.
They sent counselors who tried to convince
him that he had slipped over the edge; that
he was out of touch with reality. They
told him that women would never be

interested in him.

I laid there and thought of how they had humiliated him. I thought of how they stigmatized him and caused even his fellow prisoners to scorn and poke fun at him. All because he misinterpreted the sexual signals of the female guards. All because he desperately needed to be needed.

I thought about women in prison. I thought about them being near physically, but distant socially. I laid there thinking about the love we are denied. "If Caesar would give us access to our women," I thought, "we would leave his alone." I thought of the stress Caesar creates by torturing us with sexual deprivation. He denies us the expression of our love, puts his women nearby, and then accuses us of "hallucinations" and "delusions." The anxiety created by these thoughts pulled me back to the physical stress I was now experiencing.

I concentrated on my muscles. Every muscle in me quivered. And a few, here and there, were pulled so tightly they were partially paralyzed. All the affected muscles were on the right side of my body. I shifted my concentration to my left side. I thought of nothing else but the left side, and as I did the right side of my body began to spasm. I kept my mind buried into my left side and let the right side continuously spasm out the trapped energy. The trick was to forget that one side existed so it could relax.

Step by step I went through the ritual of commanding the release of tension. First I went through my legs, hips, stomach, chest,

and then my neck. Then I turned to my
head and played the same game with my face.
I went to my eyes, nose, mouth, forehead,
and chin. Eventually, step by step, I relaxed
every muscle in my body. It was like being
jammed up and frozen inside an iceberg and
then making each muscle thaw by controlling
the flowing radiation of my energy. Slowly,
as the last spasm disappeared in my face,
I completely relaxed. My muscles were now
calm. All the twitching was gone and I
breathed deeply and easily. I drifted into
a deep sleep.

     I awoke to the sound of a loud bell.
In my nakedness I jumped up and grabbed
my towel, soap, shampoo, and washcloth.
I wrapped the towel around me as I stood
in front of the cell door. I stood there
waiting for it to open so I could take my
shower. When the guard pulled the lever that
slid the bar from across my door and unlocked
it, I stepped into the block corridor. I
headed toward the shower but immediately
realized my behavior was out of
synchronization with what was going on
around me. Inmates were coming to their
cells instead of walking toward the shower.
They were clothed. I looked up at the dirty
windows. It was dark outside. "Damnit, I
missed the showers," I thought as I walked
back into my cell to look at my watch. I
had slept for six hours. Not only did I miss
the showers but I missed the supper bell as
well. I told myself that I must be working
too hard to sleep so long and so deeply.
It was nine o'clock at night and time to be

locked into the cell for the rest of the night. "Damnit," I thought. "I'm really dirty." I sat down on my bed waiting for the guard to come by and lock my cell door.

Another bell rang and I stood up and walked over to stand in front of the door. We had to do this twice a day. At five in the evening and at nine at night we had to stand by our cell door and let the guard come by and count us. They had to make sure no one was missing, or dead. I stood there waiting. "Damnit, I'm going to be up all night," I thought. The guard locked my door and counted me. Now I was locked in twice. They locked my door and they slid a bolt across my door and locked that also.

I waited for about twenty minutes watching to see if all the guards were gone. Once they were gone, I raised up from my bed and hung my heavy coat over the cell door again. This was against the rules, but I did it anyway so I could gain some privacy. I didn't want the guards to see me taking my bath. To them it would look crazy; I didn't need any complications. They live in a different world and just don't understand these types of things.

I got out two state-issued towels and placed them on the floor around my toilet. I cleaned up the sink and washed out the toilet real well. My sink was directly above the toilet and I stepped inside so I could take a shower. There was no way I could wait until tomorrow before I showered. I was filthy from the day's activities and I needed to get the sweat and dirt cleared from the

DEHUMANIZATION

By

Buddy Martin

pores in my flesh.

I stood in the toilet and used a large plastic container to dip into the sink. I poured the water over my head. It ran down my body and into the toilet. As the water ran down my body and into the toilet I thought of how I had changed and adapted to this strange world. Things I once ridiculed and scoffed at were now accepted without question.

I bathed my whole body this way. I then shaved, washed my face, and mopped up a little water that splashed onto the floor. I tidied up my cell and then sat down feeling clean and relaxed. I smoked a cigarette and began to plan my endeavors for the upcoming long night. I knew from falling into such a deep sleep earlier I would be up most of the night. I really didn't mind though because tomorrow was Sunday; I could sleep in.

I knew I had to occupy my time constructively or else I would eventually turn into a mental case. I knew that and I knew it well. I knew it from observing others who lived around me.

"There is so much human devastation around me," I thought. I have walked up and down this block a million times. I have unobtrusively let my vision penetrate into prison cells trying to perceive the living conditions of other men and how they cope and adapt to the challenges of this desolate human environment. Time after time I pulled my gaze back from those prison cells to feel the heavily drenched states of despair.

Hopelessness, helplessness, and the awesomely complex distortion of mental illness was evident everywhere. Their little square spaces were vast deserts of nothingness and they sat back in those shadows, with unbelieving eyes, looking out through the bars at a cold and insensitive world. Many were so deeply withdrawn it would take many years of loving human kindness to pull them out of their despair. The institution had some of them loaded with behavior modification drugs so they would sit quietly. When they moved, they moved in slow motion and they had a glaze across their eyes that blocked out the pain of prison. The institution drugs them so they won't be forced to contend with the wild hysteria that comes with perceiving the reality of confinement. "How many times has my mind withdrawn from the perception of the men in those cells with a feeling of horror?" I wondered.

I looked around my cell at my own personal comfort. My child had stolen paint from the prison's paint shop. He stole four different colors and painted my walls into sections of space that created a feeling of being larger than they really were. He painted the ceiling a dull-gray white so the light wouldn't bounce or glare. Everything was neat and clean. When the guards painted the prison, they really didn't care. They slopped one color over the walls, usually a cool blue that makes you feel emotionally like you are dwelling inside an ice cube. It is a cold gravity color. That's why I stole my own paint and created my own

environment.   If   need   be,   I   take   the
consequences.   But   I   need   to   control;   I   need
a   warm   and   loving   environment.   That   is   my
nature.   It helps me survive.

I   looked   at   my   stereo   and   color   T.V.
Ron   helped   me   pay   for   them.   We   worked
together   to   make   the   payments.   I   looked
at   the   rugs   on   my   floor   and   at   the   stolen
silk   curtains   hanging   at   the   front   of   my
cell.   I   have   beautiful   wooden   shelves   on   the
walls.   I   had   them   made   and   stole   them   from
the   wood   shop.   My   cell   looks   like   a   modern
little   apartment.   "How   many   times   have   the
guards   ripped   the   shelves   from   my   walls?"
I   asked   myself.   As   fast   as   they   tore   them
down,   I   put   them   back   up.   As   fast   as   they
took   them,   I   stole   more.   Eventually   they
began   to   turn   their   heads   and   look   the   other
way.   Some   of   them   understand   that   I'm   just
trying   to   create   a   human   environment.   I'm
not   particularly   fond   of   being   a   thief;   but
there   are   no   alternatives.   They   label   me
as   a   criminal   when   I   do   this   because   most
of   them   don't   realize   that   I'm   only   trying
to preserve my humanity.

I   looked   up   at   the   shelves   that   held   my
large   book   collection.   "You   have   a   real   good
research   library,"   I   told   myself.   "Anything
to   do   with   anything."   My   child   looked   at
me   and   laughed.   "Those   books   saved   your
mind,"   he   said.   "Oh,   you   are   awake,"   I
responded.   "I   want   to   watch   T.V.,"   he
told me.

I   reached   over   and   clicked   on   the   color
T.V.   Instant   magic.   I   was   plugged   into   a
representation   of   the   outside   society.   My

television had a sensitive tuner and I could tune in a smut channel. If I wanted, I could watch people having sex all night long. Sometimes when watching them I became so horney and lonely that I masturbated on the state-issued towel. I squirted my tremendous power, my unborn child, all over it. And then I gave it to the institutional mice.

I spun the channel selector around to catch bits and pieces of a strange world unfolding. I sat there on the bed and watched a little bit of this and a little bit of that. I looked at the modern-looking cars, watched the news, listened to a report on the economy, and watched a country music channel. In frustration I shut the damn thing off. "There just doesn't seem to be anything I can identify with," I thought. Society seems so strange. Everything looks so bizarre. Nothing I see has a relationship to the reality I know. Everything looks like fantasy. Surely there is no real world like that.

I felt strange, alienated. In my intelligence I knew it was dangerous to feel detached from free society. But yet I couldn't prevent the feeling. I felt no bond, no association, no structure or relationship that touched my emotions or the logic of my mind. That world was different from mine and yet I cried in my love for it.

I looked up at Beverly's picture in a desperate effort to find comfort. I studied her. "She is my link to humanity," I thought. "She loves me and holds me near." I thought of our bond, the years of our struggle to hold together, and the visions of our dreams.

She is in the free world and I'm locked tightly in this dark and isolated little box. She lives in a world which is alien to me, and the world I have is alien to her. She tells me about her world and I tell her about mine. The world she has when compared with mine is so different. Similarities are difficult to find; all perspectives clash. But yet, if one has the strength, courage, and sensitivity to look beyond the shadows, we are both the same. "God, what a tremendous struggle you have given us," I thought as I glanced again at Beverly's picture.

My mind was swept up by the love she and I shared. My mind drifted through the days she and I spent in the prison visiting room looking, loving and feeling. I looked into her past, she looked into mine; together we unfolded the struggles of our lives. We desperately tried to touch each other as deeply as possible as the prison guards stared with their relentless scowls.

For years we explored. We walked, struggled, crawled, and loved our way deeper and deeper into each other. We broke through each other's defenses, we became emotionally entangled; all in the eye of Caesar's institutional camera.

I sat there and thought some more. Beverly and I try to build. We struggle to be positive and productive. In our love we are happy and we believe human beings should be like that. But there are two worlds that surround our bond. One is the free world and the other is the prison society. We are trapped in an American crisis. The visiting room is the Berlin Wall of the American prison system. It is here that prisoners and loved ones peer at one another across hundreds of years of institutional barbarism.

From time to time the prison authorities bring tours of people through the visiting room so they can view the families and the men they come to see. They are like a group of people visiting a factory and walking down the assembly line staring at the manufactured product. Everything looks so normal to them. When they walk through it just looks like people sitting in a room under normal conditions. They cannot see that our self-expression is frozen by rules. They cannot see the real human struggle.

In prison the inmate is surrounded by a dark and devastating environment. Prison officials have no time for human concern; their primary focus is containment. When loved ones come to visit, that presents an unwelcome problem. The prison administrators are ill-equipped for such functions. Security, custody, and control are primary orientations. In a maximum security prison love and caring are security hazards.

According to the rules, you can only kiss your visitor once when they come in and once when they leave. You cannot hug and touch and desire the love of another. That is against the rules. The prison administrators demand coldness. Everything is structured to forcefully rip apart any strands of human bonds that remain between inmates and those who still care. Prison officials are most comfortable when outside human contact is kept to a minimum.

Some guards who run the visiting room attempt to be humane. They do not strictly enforce visitation rules. They attempt to be sensitive and caring, but the reality of the social atmosphere makes their human concern disappear amid the sea of environmental insanity. These guards constantly run the risk of being accused of not doing their jobs.

Most people visit on weekends. On Saturdays and Sundays the visiting rooms turn into mad houses. When packed with visitors the visiting rooms are like boxcars; they stuff you in like cattle. You have to scream to be heard. Men, women and children are all packed together with each trying desperately to cram months and years of concern into a few hours of togetherness. Everyone tries to reach out and touch the other emotionally, but in this institutional setting even love and affection become twisted and distorted.

Throughout the visiting room you can observe the desperation, anger, frustration and resentment. Across the way a mom and dad sit close to their imprisoned son, talking real sincerely. Next to them a prisoner slides his hand up his wife's dress and tugs at her panties. Old friends try desperately to relive past adventures. An inmate and his minister discuss religious matters. Children are everywhere running, screaming, and exploring. All a bit uncomfortable under the guard's close surveillance. Men and women separated by years of lonely nights come together here for a few hours of visitation. They desperately struggle for an unseen touch. After all, that is all they have to sustain their relationship.

I have often been amazed at the many subtle, innovative ways devised to love and be loved in this institutional atmosphere. I have sat and watched many times the human struggle for togetherness. Beverly and I, too, are part of this struggle. We pretend to be frozen and then secretly love in the cold shadows. If we are caught we are punished and humiliated. They try to convince us that love is wrong.

Every so often the guards catch an inmate and his wife or girl friend attempting to make love. They immediately grab him, and chase her out of the institution. They humiliate and degrade her as they push her out the door. They lock the inmate in the dungeon and accuse him of perversion. This is all in stark contrast to their treatment of homosexuality.

Within the prison walls homosexuality is condoned and, in many cases, accepted. For some strange reason in the topsy-turvy world of prison social dynamics, traditional attitudes toward sex are inverted. Many guards discretely look the other way when coming upon a homosexual affair, while reacting with rage and indignation at the sight of a man and a woman making love. In prison, love becomes just one more distorted and shriveled appendage of the social body.

This prison world tears love and

commitment apart. The inmate is stripped
of all human qualities. Once branded, the
inmate is forced to live a life of emotional
desolation. All outside concern for the inmate
is discouraged. The entire prison social
structure, though disguised to look progressive
with its superficial programming, is nothing
more than a modern-day concentration camp.
The prison administrators fail to realize that
by stripping inmates emotionally naked today,
they are contributing to the violent and
destructive crimes of tomorrow.

My thoughts drifted me back into the
reality of my prison cell. I glanced back
up at Beverly's picture again. I then shifted
my gaze and glanced across other pictures
I have hanging on the hundred-year-old prison
wall. I looked at some of the snapshots of
my art and then turned my eyes to the head
of my broken bed. There I let my eyes rest
on a picture of the first watercolor I did
for Beverly. I called it, "The Garden of
Eden." I looked deeply into that work of
art and came into contact with all the
complex insights God showed me in that
creative journey. I looked into the tremendous
wonder God had given us in life. From life,
into life, through life, and then to be born
back into life again. That is God's magic
in the living cycle.

I shifted my eyes and looked on the
other wall at a painting of Caesar. An
imprisoned artist created the composition and
then gave it to me as a token of his
friendship. I looked at it closely and thought
of perversion. I thought of power and

corruption. I looked at the base character in the dark side of the human spirit and then reflected on the structure of reality which surrounded me. "Caesar makes me feel hopeless," I thought. I looked at the structure of the composition and thought of how well my friend captured the dark primitive strivings that streak their way through human nature. "He did an excellent job," I thought. I glanced back up at Beverly's picture and thought of God.

I thought of my insecure feelings as I contemplated the realities of prison. I thought of all the other men right now sitting in their prison cells. Most of the cells have two men stuffed into the space which was made too small for one. Their lives are so tightly crammed together that not only do they have to feel their own tremendous anguish and suffering, but they also have to feel and live the anguish of the one pushed up against them. They tightly rub against each other in that little box. Many of them, in their emotional confusion, get lost in the deprived perceptions and turn to rape. Somebody has to be a girl. Somebody has to be a wife.

Most of the men are trapped in a primitive state of ignorance. About half of the prison population has a reading level below the eighth grade. The average achievement level is that of a sixth grade child. These men have the minds of children and they are involved in a desperate struggle to survive in this exceedingly complex jungle. Their decisions are based mainly on instinct and they have no constructive model to guide them. Not only must they contend with their own ignorance, but they must successfully compete to survive among the ignorance which surrounds them. They live in a world that is competitive, violent, and insanely frightening.

Under such conditions the very idea of rehabilitation is a joke. It is true that constructive educational and vocational programs are available. But without the background, motivation, or guidance to develop constructive pursuits, the average inmate is more concerned with simple day-to-day survival. Without a firm foundation it is impossible to build a constructive future. The destructive and violent adaptations learned in the streets and in the many reformatories and juvenile homes form the social base that is extended, exaggerated, and, on the part of the prison officials, even expected in a maximum security prison. Unless an inmate finds reason to make a sharp and dramatic break with his past, he becomes hopelessly caught up in the violence and destructiveness of the prison environment.

But not all men are so primitive or destructively aggressive. There are not many, but there are a few who have established positive goals and orientations. Right now they sit in their cells attempting to figure out how they can possibly salvage their lives. They look around at the horrifying darkness and attempt to creatively produce some assemblage of constructive light. They know they need it to salvage their mental spirit

and warm their soul.   This world is so dark.
It's a world where positive and constructive
pursuits are looked on with suspicion.   It's
a world where both inmates and administrative
personnel   punish,   rather   than   reward
accomplishment.

Over   the   years   I've   closely   observed
prison   counselors   as   they   interact   with
inmates.   Never in my life have I observed
such tremendous depths of insensitivity.   There
is nothing but pure hatred and condemnation
that radiates from the spirit of their guidance.
They   belittle,   humiliate,   condemn,   deceive,
and betray.   They treat inmates as if they
were subhuman.   The inmate, to the average
counselor, is no more than an outlet which
can   help   them   unleash   their   pent-up
frustrations and aggressions.   The inmate is
their whipping post and they let him know
quite   clearly   that   they   perceive   him   as
despicable.   The entire thrust of a counseling
session is to let the inmate know he is
worthless.   They let you know that they feel
you should not bother them because they have
more important concerns.   And they sting
your   emotions   so   you   won't   bother   them
again.

The counselors have abandoned the prison
inmate.   They think inmates to be hopeless
cases.   Of course, there are one or two
good counselors here and there, but they are
so few that they are difficult to find.   I've
questioned them about their behavior and they
dismiss it with counselor language.   They call
it "burn out."   "After you hear so many
problems you don't wish to hear any more,"

they say. So to keep you away, they abuse you knowing full well you will not be back again. In the prison system counselors and many of the treatment staff are among the highest forms of social disgrace. In their treatment of inmates, many of them are manipulative, self-centered, arrogrant and destructive. Even prison guards are more perceptive and sensitive than counselors.

I once again focused on my prison cell. I glanced around at the little square world in which I live. I attempted to perceive the stark reality of it so I could fully appreciate the intensity of my desire to be free. I felt my child's restless soul come alive. There was a feeling of isolated panic buried somewhere deep in my psyche. To gain a positive and productive perspective I shoved his anguish back into a far corner of the unconscious portion of my brain many years ago. But just like a repressed Freudian desire, the demand for justice and freedom frequently forces its way into consciousness. My child knows that he has been unjustly imprisoned. He feels like he has been buried alive.

Sometimes he feels like running, screaming, and tearing at the walls. In his feelings of desperation, he feels like clawing at the bricks with his bare fingers. At times I have to stop him from scratching, tearing, and ripping at this dark world. Sometimes his desperation is so great I think he will scream out with such intensity that he will disturb the molecules on the other side of the universe. He prays that someone will hear his cry and, in the name of justice, tear down the iron gate that keeps him in this dark world. He looks for a link, an allegiance with humanity. He knows that is the only way he can break the cycle of alienation and the cold feeling of isolated deprivation. Society has the key that will either set him free, or lock him forever in this man-made hell.

Slowly I looked around at the little square box in which I live. I didn't want to miss a thing. I wanted to feel it all, to pull its darkness deep inside of me and touch the depth of despair. I wanted to feel every state of insecurity and every threat to my existence. I sat there and thought of this gladiator world. Again I glanced over at the large envelope I received from Ted. It laid

The   Marble   Palace

there on the old wooden desk, just waiting
for my response. "I wonder what I can
achieve with that?" I thought to myself.

I looked up on the wall at the picture
of Beverly and I thought of the tremendous
challenges that face our love. "God, can
we really build a future for our love? Can
we really be successful?" I wondered. I sat
there on the bed thinking of failure. "I have
failed all my life," was the current of my
thoughts. "I feel like I've been buried here
forever, isolated and separated from humanity.
I've struggled anyway. God, is my desire
to become a successful man just an illusionary
dream?"

I sat there thinking about wasted efforts,
frivilous ambitions, and the very real
possibility that I could destroy Beverly by
pulling her deep into the heart of my dreams.
"If I fail, it could destroy her," I thought.
She loves me and dedicates her life to me.
"If I die here, or fail here, what will it
do to her life?" I wondered what such a
tremendous tragedy would do to the spirit
of her existence. At times I strongly sense
the possibility of her lying collapsed and
broken upon the ground.

A strong part of my character has
the impulse to push her away. From time
to time I have the tendency to chase her
from these dark walls and tell her I don't
love her. I believe that pain would force
her to never return. I know that emotion
would shatter her. But, too, she would heal
and then rebuild a future that could be more
productive. Maybe she should find a man

in the free world who will love her?

And, too, in that dilemma, I know if I deny love I will drive myself into the deepest form of alienation. If I deny love I deny my own humanity. If I deny love, if I deny Beverly, I deny the bond that links me to the world. And, too, I know that a future for our love is a gamble. Our destiny is so uncertain and the possibilities of success are weighed heavily against us. I am so afraid loving me will destroy her.

I am trapped in so many ways. Can I accept her love, accept the challenges that come with that love, face the possibility of failing with that love, or feel the emotional devastation that may come in the loss of that love? Or, in a state of love, should I reject that love and accept the cold state of alienation?

Again I looked over at the envelope Ted sent me. I began to think, "Perhaps the beginning of a positive and constructive future is lying there." I looked up at Beverly's picture again. I came into contact with this overwhelming feeling of love I felt for her. I thought of all the times she made me promise I'd try real hard to be set free. Time and time and time again she made me promise I wouldn't give up and that I would believe in our love. "She said she needed me," I thought.

I stared at Beverly's picture for about five minutes and then I reached up and pulled it from the wall. I ran my fingers sensitively across the image of her breasts. In that moment I heard her laughing in my spirit.

I hung her picture back upon the one hundred year old wall where she could look at me and guard me. "OK, Sweetie," I said to her with my heart, "we'll give it a try."

I reached over and grabbed the envelope. I pulled out the documents and scattered them across my bed. I looked for the rough draft of "Caesar's Gladiator Pit." "Let me write down a few notes," I said to myself as I glanced around at my cold and desolate cell.

"Early I woke to the sound of loud screaming noise. The shadows in my prison cell were still darkly blended together as I felt the anguish of awareness . . . ."

JOURNEY THROUGH THE SUN

By

Buddy Martin